بسم الله الرحمن الرحيم

English Edition published in October 2006

Published by:
Ta-Ha Publishers Ltd.
1 Wynne Road
London SW9 OBB
United Kingdom

Website: http://www.taha.co.uk
E-Mail: sales@ taha.co.uk

By Adem Yakup
Translated By: Ron Evans
Edited By: Abdassamad Clarke

ISBN
1 842000 78 0

Printed and bound by:
Secil Ofset in İstanbul
Address: 100. Mahallesi MAS-SIT Matbaacılar Sitesi
4. Cadde No:77 Bağcılar- İstanbul / TURKEY

Website: http://www.ademyakup.com
www.bookglobal.net

Ta-Ha Publishers Ltd.
1 Wynne Road London SW9 OBB

THE MIRACLES OF THE PROPHET MUHAMMAD ﷺ

ADEM YAKUP

October, 2006

CONTENTS

THE MIRACLES OF THE PROPHET MUHAMMAD ﷺ

1. Introduction

Throughout history, Allah has sent messengers to every nation showing them the Straight Path, in order for people to achieve good in this world and the next. The Qur'an tells us that this is a great mercy for all those who believe:

Allah showed great kindness to the believers when He sent a messenger to them from among themselves to recite His signs to them and purify them and teach them the Book and Wisdom, even though before that they were clearly misguided. (Surah Al 'Imran: 164)

And Allah said to His Messenger, Muhammad ﷺ:

We have only sent you as a mercy to all the worlds. (Surat al-Anbiya': 107)

These messengers were guiding lights for the communities to which they were sent; they showed their people the Right Path and imparted to them the commands of Allah. They conveyed the importance of believing in Allah and following His commands in order to achieve success in the Hereafter. However, throughout history, few people have heeded or appreciated what a great mercy these messengers were for them as highlighted in the Qur'an:

… But most people have no faith. (Surat ar-Ra'd: 1)

But most people, for all your eagerness, are not believers. (Surah Yusuf: 103)

The sole purpose of these messengers was to spread the Word of Allah. They wanted no material recompense for their work, desiring only the pleasure of Allah. They were people of noble character and genuine fear of Allah *(taqwa)*. As well as receiving no material benefit from their work, they also experienced great difficulties and were tried in various ways in their attempt to bring people to faith. But these apparent difficulties only served to increase their faith and dedication even more. In return for their devotion, faithfulness, steadfastness, sincerity and trust in Him, Allah helped and supported His messengers, as He says in the Qur'an:

Allah has written, 'I will be victorious, I and My messengers.' Allah is Most Strong, Almighty. (Surat al-Mujadalah: 21)

Allah helped His messengers and those who believed with material and spiritual strength against the unbelievers who wished to harm them. He increased the abundance of blessings He bestowed on them and provided an escape from every difficulty. He increased their courage and strength in every hardship, lightened their burdens and strengthened their resolve by reminding them of His mercy. Allah tells us in the Qur'an of the support and protection He gives to His prophets and the believers who follow them:

We will certainly help Our messengers and those who believe both in the life of this world and on the Day the witnesses appear. (Surah Ghafir: 51)

Allah also supported some of His messengers by granting them miracles. A miracle *(mu'jizah)* involves a challenge from Allah to His creation. It is something that human beings are not capable of doing by themselves; it can only be done by the will of Allah. Miracles, by their very nature, are extraordinary events and so they have a tremendous effect on people. They had the twofold effect of strengthening the resolve and faith of those who already believed, while causing many unbelievers to come to faith. Those who did not believe were challenged to produce something like it and when they were unable to do this, Allah's message was supported and the weakness of the unbelievers was exposed.

The Miracles that Allah Granted the Prophets

In the Qur'an there are detailed accounts of the lives of the prophets, of the miracles with which Allah strengthened their faith and supported their message; and of the miracles He gave them as protection against the deniers. Prophets Ibrahim عليه السلام, Musa عليه السلام, 'Isa عليه السلام and Prophet Muhammad ﷺ were among some of the messengers to whom Allah granted miracles, some of which are highlighted below.

The Miracles granted to Ibrahim عليه السلام

The fire that Ibrahim عليه السلام was thrown into became cool:

The idol worshippers were angry with Ibrahim عليه السلام as he had criticised their gods, so they plotted to throw him into the fire, but Allah protected His messenger by a miracle. Allah tells us in the Qur'an that, at His command, the flames did not harm Ibrahim عليه السلام:

> We said, 'Fire, be coolness and peace for Ibrahim!' (Surat al-Anbiya': 69)

The birds that Ibrahim عليه السلام had cut into pieces came back to him alive:

> When Ibrahim said, 'My Lord, show me how You bring the dead to life.' He asked, 'Do you not then have faith?' He replied, 'Indeed I do! But so that my heart may be at peace.' He said, 'Take four birds and train them to yourself. Then put a part of them on each mountain and call to them; they will come rushing to you. Know that Allah is Almighty, All-Wise.' (Surat al-Baqarah: 260)

The Miracles granted to Musa عليه السلام

Musa عليه السلام was granted miracles by Allah which he used to invite Pharaoh and his courtiers to the Right Path.

Musa's رود turned into a serpent and swallowed the ruses of the magicians:

He said, 'If you have come with a Clear Sign produce it if you are telling the truth.' So He threw down his staff and there it was, unmistakably a snake. (Surat al-A'raf: 106-107)

'Throw down what is in your right hand. It will swallow up their handiwork. Their handiwork is just a magician's trick. Magicians do not prosper wherever they go.' (Surah Ta Ha: 69)

Musa's هand became as white as snow:

'Put your hand under your arm and press it to your side. It will emerge pure white yet quite unharmed, another Sign. In this way We show you some of Our greatest Signs.' (Surah Ta Ha: 22-23)

As Musa and the Bani Isra'il fled from Pharaoh and his people, a miracle of Allah allowed them to escape unharmed while the deniers perished:

Musa struck the sea with his rod and a way opened through it:

And when the two hosts came into sight of one another Musa's companions said, 'We will surely be overtaken!' He said, 'Never! My Lord is with me and He will guide me.' So We revealed to Musa, 'Strike the sea with your staff.' And it split in two, each part like a towering cliff. And We brought the others right up to it. We rescued Musa and all those who were with him. Then We drowned the rest. (Surat ash-Shu'ara': 61-66)

The Miracle granted to Yunus

Yunus was miraculously saved after being swallowed by a fish:

Yunus too was one of the Messengers. When he ran away to the fully laden ship and cast lots and lost. Then the fish devoured him and he was to blame. Had it not been that he was a man who glorified Allah, he would have remained inside its belly until the Day they are raised again. So We cast him up onto the beach and he was sick. (Surat as-Saffat: 139-145)

The Miracle granted to Zakariyya ﷺ

Zakariyya ﷺ was told he would have a child in his old age:

> Then and there Zakariyya called on his Lord and said, 'O Lord, grant me by Your favour an upright child. You are the Hearer of Prayer.' The angels called out to him while he was standing in prayer in the Upper Room: 'Allah gives you the good news of Yahya, who will come to confirm a Word from Allah, and will be a leader and a celibate, a Prophet and one of the right-acting.' He said, 'My Lord, how can I possibly have a son when I have reached old age and my wife is barren?' He said, 'It will be so. Allah does whatever He wills.' (Surah Al 'Imran: 38-40)

The Miracle granted to Maryam

Maryam always had food with her:

> … Every time Zakariyya visited her in the Upper Room, he found food with her. He said, 'Maryam, how did you come by this?' She said, 'It is from Allah. Allah provides for whoever He wills without any reckoning.' (Surah Al 'Imran: 37)

The Miracles granted to 'Isa ﷺ

'Isa ﷺ was granted miracles from the time of his birth and throughout his life, which have been detailed in the Qur'an:

Remember when Allah said, "Isa, son of Maryam, remember My blessing to you and to your mother when I reinforced you with the Purest Ruh so that you could speak to people in the cradle and when you were fully grown; and when I taught you the Book and Wisdom, and the Torah and the Injil; and when you created a bird-shape out of clay by My permission, and then breathed into it and it became a bird by My permission; and healed the blind and the leper by My permission; and when you brought forth the dead by My permission; and when I held back the tribe of Israel from you, when you brought them the Clear Signs and those of them who were kafir said, "This is nothing but downright magic".' (Surat al-Ma'idah: 110)

He [Allah] will teach him ['Isa] the Book and Wisdom, and the Torah and the Injil, as a Messenger to the tribe of Israel, saying: 'I have brought you a Sign from your Lord. I will create the shape of a bird out of clay for you and then breathe into it and it will be a bird by Allah's permission. I will heal the blind and the leper, and bring the dead to life, by Allah's permission. I will tell you what you eat and what you store up in your homes. There is a Sign for you in that if you are believers.' (Surah Al 'Imran: 48-49)

There are many other miracles mentioned in the Qur'an besides those outlined above. These and other miracles all occur by the command of Allah and in the way He wills. In the Qur'an, Allah says:

We sent Messengers before you and gave them wives and children. Nor was any Messenger able to bring a Sign except by Allah's permission. There is a prescribed limit to every term. (Surat ar-Ra'd: 38)

The Prophet Muhammad ﷺ was a blessed individual whom Allah made a model for all people in his goodness, strong faith and in his every word and action. As with previous prophets and messengers, the Prophet Muhammad ﷺ was also granted miracles throughout his life for people to see and learn from, by Allah's permission. Only the Companions witnessed some of these miracles but great numbers of those who denied the Prophet ﷺ witnessed others.

An account of some of the Prophet's miracles has come down to us in the Qur'an. We know of others through the hadith of the Prophet ﷺ and by various writings of Islamic scholars. Through these sources, it is possible to see the miraculous aspects of this blessed man who was sent as a mercy to the world and to understand the importance of using the Qur'an and the Sunnah of the Prophet ﷺ as guides in our everyday life.

2. The Miracles that Allah Granted to the Prophet Muhammad ﷺ prior to Prophethood

According to historical texts, Muhammad ﷺ was given the honour of being a prophet when he was forty years old. But, before he received any revelations, certain miraculous events took place in his life that gave indications as to his future.

The midwife present at his birth, ash-Shifa, the mother of the famed companion 'Abdur-Rahman ibn 'Awf, said that when the Prophet ﷺ was born into her hands and sneezed, she heard someone say 'May Allah have mercy on you!' and she stated that the entire horizon became illuminated (Abu Nu'aym).

The Prophet ﷺ was always shaded when he travelled. Khadijah ؆ mentioned that she saw two angels shading her husband while he travelled (Ibn Sa'd), while Halima, his foster-mother among the desert tribe of Bani Sa'd ibn Bakr, said that she saw a cloud shade him while he was with her. Once while the Prophet ﷺ was on a journey, he sat down under a dry tree to rest. The tree grew and spread out and according to some traditions, the shadow of the tree inclined towards the Prophet ﷺ to shade him. The area surrounding the tree also became lush and green.

Nearing the time of his Prophethood, the dreams that the Prophet ﷺ saw in his sleep foreshadowed things that were to come true. According to hadith, these dreams occurred over a period of about six months. The eminent Islamic scholar, Imam al-Bukhari, gives an account of these dreams in his collection.

The Miracles that Allah Granted to the Prophet Muhammad ﷺ prior to Prophethood

Aisha ☙ narrated: 'The first thing with which the revelation began for the Messenger of Allah ﷺ was correct dreams in sleep. He never saw a dream but that it came like the breaking of the dawn.' (Al-Bukhari)

Islamic scholars explain that the reason for the dreams coming true in this manner was to prepare Muhammad ﷺ in his sleep for the great responsibility of prophethood.

3. The Miracle of the Revelation

Undoubtedly, the greatest miracle that was granted to the Prophet Muhammad ﷺ was Allah's revelation of the Qur'an to him. The Prophet ﷺ was chosen by Allah to impart His message to mankind. This was a great responsibility, as the Qur'an outlines:

> You who are enwrapped in your clothing! Stay up at night, except a little, half of it, or a little less, or a little more, and recite the Qur'an distinctly. We will impose a weighty Word upon you. Certainly rising at night has a stronger effect and is more conducive to concentration. In the daytime much of your time is taken up by business matters. Remember the Name of your Lord, and devote yourself to Him completely. (Surat al-Muzzammil: 1-8)

The Revelation

The first revelation came soon after Muhammad ﷺ began seeing the true dreams. It was because of these dreams that he had started to retreat to *Ghar Hira'* (the cave of Hira') on *Jabal an-Nur* (the Mountain of Light) about twelve kilometres from Makkah. While he was alone in the cave during the month of Ramadan, when the Prophet ﷺ was forty years of age, the angel Jibril appeared to him and asked him to recite. These events are fully described in the hadith:

> *Aisha ﵂ narrated: The first thing with which the revelation began for the Messenger of Allah ﷺ was correct dreams in sleep. He never saw a dream but that it came like the breaking of the dawn. He used to go in seclusion to (the cave of) Hira' where he used to worship (Allah alone)*

continuously for many nights. He used to take provision with him for that (stay) and then like-wise come back to Khadijah to take his food again for another period. Then suddenly the Truth descended upon him while he was in the cave of Hira'. The angel came to him in it and asked him to read.

The Prophet replied, 'I do not know how to read.' (The Prophet added), 'The angel caught me (forcefully) and pressed me so hard that I could not bear it anymore. He then released me and again asked me to read, and I replied, "I do not know how to read," whereupon he caught me again and pressed me a second time till I could not bear it anymore. He then released me and asked me again to read, but again I replied, "I do not know how to read (or, what shall I read?)." Thereupon he caught me for the third time and pressed me and then released me and said, "Read: In the Name of your Lord, Who has created. Has created man from a clot. Read and Your Lord is Most Generous ... that which he knew not." (Surat al-'Alaq: 1-5)' Then Allah's Messenger returned with it... (Al-Bukhari)

There are also a number of verses in the Qur'an that describe the Prophet's ﷺ encounter with Jibril and the revelation of the Qur'an to him:

Your companion is not misguided or misled; nor does he speak from whim. It is nothing but Revelation revealed, taught him by one immensely strong. Possessing power and splendour. He stood there stationary – there on the highest horizon. Then he drew near and hung suspended. He was two bow-lengths away or even closer. Then He revealed to His slave what He revealed. His heart did not lie about what he saw. What! Do you dispute with him about what he saw? (Surat an-Najm: 2-12)

According to some interpretations of the Qur'an, these verses refer to the revelation of the Qur'an, however, some other interpretations take these verses to refer to the *Mi'raj* (ascent through the heavens).

Several other verses attest to the fact that it was Jibril who delivered the Qur'an from Allah to the Prophet ﷺ. In these verses Jibril is also referred to as 'The Purest *Ruh*' or 'The Faithful *Ruh*.'

Say: 'Anyone who is the enemy of Jibril should know that it was he who brought it down upon your heart, by Allah's authority, confirming what came before, and as guidance and good news for the believers.' (Surat al-Baqarah: 97)

Say: 'The Purest Ruh has brought it down from your Lord with truth, to make those who have iman firm, and as guidance and good news for the Muslims.' (Surat an-Nahl: 102)

Truly it is revelation sent down by the Lord of all the worlds. The Faithful Ruh brought it down to your heart so you would be one of the Warners. (Surat ash-Shu'ara': 192-194)

This last verse shows that the Qur'an was revealed right to the heart of the Prophet ❊. This was a mercy from Allah to the Prophet ❊ as Allah says in the Qur'an:

But [We allowed the revelation to remain and endure] as a mercy from your Lord. His favour to you is indeed immense. (Surat al-Isra': 87)

You did not expect to be given the Book. It is nothing but a mercy from your Lord... (Surat al-Qasas: 86)

After the first verses were revealed, there is a tradition that the revelations to the Prophet ❊ ceased for a certain time. The hadith tell us that, when the revelations resumed, the next set of verses received were the first verses of Surat al-Muddaththir:

You who are enveloped in your cloak! Arise and warn. Magnify your Lord. (Surat al-Muddaththir: 1-3)

After receiving these verses, the Prophet ❊ obeyed this command from Allah and assumed his responsibility of proclaiming the revelation. The Prophet ❊ continued to receive Divine Revelation from this time until his death, twenty-three years later.

The State of the Prophet ﷺ While He was Receiving Revelation

There are descriptions in the hadith of what it was like for the Prophet ﷺ to receive revelation. For example, when the revelations came, those present with the Prophet ﷺ report that they heard a sound like the buzzing of bees. Some sources say that there was a sound like a bee buzzing around the Prophet's ﷺ face. A number of hadith describe the state of the Prophet while he was receiving revelation.

> *Aisha ◈ narrated: Al-Harith ibn Hisham ◈ asked the Prophet ﷺ, 'How does the revelation come to you?' He replied, 'In all of that the angel comes to me, sometimes with a voice that resembles the sound of a ringing bell, and when this state abandons me, I remember what the angel has said, and this type of revelation is the hardest on me; and sometimes the angel comes to me in the shape of a man and talks to me, and I understand and remember what he says.' (Al-Bukhari)*

> *Aisha ◈ narrated: 'I saw the Prophet ﷺ receiving revelation on a very cold day and noticed the sweat dropping from his forehead.' (Al-Bukhari and At-Tirmidhi)*

> *Zayd ibn Thabit ◈ narrated: 'I wrote the revelations from Allah to the Prophet ﷺ. When the revelation came to him he felt a great weariness and had beads of sweat like pearls. When the state of revelation ended he recited, and I would write.' (At-Tabarani) [1]*

> *Abu Hurayrah ◈ narrated: 'When the revelation came from Allah to the Prophet ﷺ it was as if he had fainted.' (Abu Nu'aym) [2]*

1 As-Suyuti, *Tahdhib al-khasa'is al-nabawiyyah al-kubra* (The Awesome Characteristics of the Prophet [saas]), Iz Publication, Istanbul, 2003, p. 298
2 *Ibid.*, p. 300

The Qur'an was Revealed to the Heart of the Prophet ⹅

Allah revealed the Qur'an in stages over a period of twenty-three years, right to the heart of the Prophet Muhammad ⹅:

> Those who are kafir say, 'Why was the Qur'an not sent down to him all in one go?' It is so that We can fortify your heart by it. We have recited it distinctly little by little. (Surat al-Furqan: 32)

Throughout the period of revelation, Allah supported His Prophet ⹅ and helped him to impart His message correctly to people. Allah advised the Prophet ⹅ about how to recite the Qur'an:

> Do not move your tongue trying to hasten it. Its collection and recitation are Our affair. So when We recite it, follow its recitation. Then its explanation is Our concern. (Surat al-Qiyamah: 16-19)

> High exalted be Allah, the King, the Real! Do not rush ahead with the Qur'an before its revelation to you is complete, and say: 'My Lord, increase me in knowledge.' (Surah Ta Ha: 114)

He also helped the Prophet ⹅ to commit the verses to memory:

> We will cause you to recite so that you do not forget. (Surat al-A'la: 6)

The ability of the Prophet's ⹅ to learn all the verses of the Qur'an in this way was another miracle that Allah gave to him. It made the *da'wah* work of the Prophet ⹅ easier by his being able to recall the verses when he needed to:

> We will ease you to the Easy Way. (Surat al-A'la: 8)

It was also Allah's way of protecting the Qur'an and ensuring that it could not be distorted or forgotten, a miracle that continues down to this day with the enormous numbers of people who commit the Qur'an to memory *(huffaz)*.

> Recite what has been revealed to you of your Lord's Book. No one can change His Words. You will never find any safe haven apart from Him. (Surat al-Kahf: 27)

4. The Miracle of the Qur'an

The Qur'an is the Word of Allah revealed for all humanity, for all time. The reasons that the Qur'an can be considered a miracle are too numerous in themselves to be listed. However, there are three main reasons that distinguish the Qur'an as a miracle: its literary excellence, its content and its protection by Allah.

The Literary Excellence of the Qur'an

The Qur'an was revealed in Arabic to the Arabs as explained in the Qur'an:

If We had made it a Qur'an in a foreign tongue they would have said, 'Why have its Signs not been made plain? What! A foreign language for an Arab?' (Surah Fussilat: 44)

In order to better understand the literary excellence of the Qur'an, it is necessary to learn about the language of the Arabs to whom the Qur'an was revealed. In Arabia, before the advent of Islam, poetry and literature were highly developed. There were stunningly original poets and fluent and eloquent individuals who used the Arabic language superlatively well. The literary men of a tribe were considered on a par with the people's greatest heroes. Because of the importance placed on literature and rhetoric, the *Mu'allaqat* (seven odes written by seven poets) were written in gold letters and suspended on the walls of the Ka'bah. [3] Some of them were recited to the people on great occasions such as the fair at Ukkaz. Even the Bedouin nomads could sometimes give recitations of poetry as good as or better than any composed by poets in the cities and people would be moved by their recitations. [4]

3 'Mu'allaqat': http://www.britannica.com/eb/article-9054111
4 Ahmet Cevdet Pasa, Muallim Mahir iz, *Peygamber Efendimiz (sav)* (Our Prophet [saas]), Izmir, Isik Publications, 1996, pp. 55-56

Therefore, it was at that time, when eloquence and style of language were well developed, that the Qur'an was revealed. As the Prophet ﷺ recited the Qur'an to the unbelievers of Makkah, even these literary individuals could not fail to be impressed by it. Some people converted to Islam simply on hearing the beautiful verses – most famously Umar ibn al-Khattab ﷺ, who was one of the fiercest opponents of Islam, converted to Islam upon reading the first verses of Surah Ta-Ha.

Some people did not embrace Islam upon hearing the Qur'an, but they could not find a response to it. The unbelievers mocked the Prophet ﷺ accusing him of writing the Qur'an himself:

> **Those who are kafir say, 'This is nothing but a lie he has invented and other people have helped him to do it. They have brought injustice and falsehood.' (Surat al-Furqan: 4)**

> **They say, 'It is myths of previous peoples which he has had transcribed and which are read out to him in the morning and the evening.' (Surat al-Furqan: 5)**

Allah gave the wisest response to the elaborately decorated rhetoric of the Arabs, and to their most famous poets and finest orators, and presented to them the challenge of producing something like it.

> **If you have doubts about what We have sent down to Our slave, produce another surah equal to it, and call your witnesses, besides Allah, if you are telling the truth. (Surat al-Baqarah: 23)**

> **Do they say, 'He has invented it'? Say: 'Then produce a surah like it and call on anyone you can besides Allah if you are telling the truth.' (Surah Yunus: 38)**

But Allah knows that no-one can or ever will be able to achieve this:

> **Say: 'If both men and jinn banded together to produce the like of this Qur'an, they could never produce anything like it, even if they backed each other up.' (Surat al-Isra': 88)**

> **Or do they say, 'He has invented it?' Say, 'Then produce ten**

invented surahs like this, and call on anyone you can besides Allah if you are telling the truth.' If they do not respond to you then know that it has been sent down with Allah's knowledge and that there is no god but Him. So will you not become Muslims? (Surah Hud: 13-14)

Do they say, 'He has invented it'? Say: 'Then produce a surah like it and call on anyone you can besides Allah if you are telling the truth.' No, the fact is that they have denied something which their knowledge does not embrace and the meaning of which has not yet reached them. In the same way those before them also denied the truth. See the final fate of the wrongdoers! (Surah Yunus: 38-39)

The great Islamic thinker, Bediuzzaman Said Nursi says of the impact of the revelation of the Qur'an on the Arabs:

When the Qur'an came, it challenged at the same time the experts in these four fields. First, it made the men of eloquence bow down before it. They all listened to it with amazement. Second, it stunned the poets and orators so that they bit their fingers in astonishment. Their most beautiful poems written in gold were given a blow, and the famous Seven Poems that were placed on the walls of the Ka'bah as an object of pride were brought down. Third, it also silenced the soothsayers and magicians, made them forget about their discoveries of hidden knowledge, resulted in the expulsion of the jinn from the heavens, and brought the process of divination to a certain end. Fourth, it rescued from myth and fabrications those who were cognisant of the events of bygone times and the facts of cosmology, teaching them the real story of past events and the illuminating knowledge of the facts of creation. Thus did those four groups bow down before the Qur'an in astonishment and respect and become its students. None of them ever dared dispute with a single verse of it. [5]

---

5 Bediuzzaman Said Nursi, *Risale-i Nur Collection*, "The Letters: The Nineteenth Letter, Eighteenth Sign, Second Remark", http://www.risale-inur.com.tr/rnk/eng/letters/19letter.html

The Qur'an is written in such a way that no human being could ever reproduce anything like it. The Arabic language itself is very pure; it is not like the Arabic language spoken by Arabs today. The Qur'an gives its message clearly and concisely, yet eloquently. Numerous metaphors and expressions are used to make clear the message of the Qur'an.

We have variegated throughout this Qur'an all kinds of examples for people, but, more than anything else, man is argumentative! (Surat al-Kahf: 54)

It is a book of great depth and layers of meanings. However, even a superficial read of the Qur'an will reveal that there are a limited number of words (some two thousand) in the whole of the Qur'an which have been used to convey a vast range of commands, concepts and facts. It is this repetition that makes the Book easy to understand and to remember by those who read it:

And We have indeed made the Qur'an easy to understand and remember… (Surat al-Qamar: 17)

Yet despite apparent repetition of key themes, the Qur'an never feels repetitive and even if one reads it repeatedly throughout one's lifetime one can never fail to appreciate its elegance or tire of reading it.

Allah has sent down the Supreme Discourse, a Book consistent in its frequent repetitions. (Surat az-Zumar: 23)

The Content of the Qur'an

The Qur'an is unique in its content because it is a Divine revelation. It contains guidance from Allah for all mankind; it helps people to recognise their own selves; it gives information about the past and the future that no human beings or spirits could know; and all it reveals is true. In addition, some scientific matters that have only recently come to light with the aid of twentieth and twenty-first century technology were alluded to in the Qur'an some 1400 years ago.

With the sublime wisdom it contains, the truth it reveals about the past and the future and its revelations that dispel ignorance and uncover the secrets of human dispositions, the Qur'an has no equal. Its miraculous character is relevant to all human beings that have been and will be created. Its commands and prohibitions are valid until the Day of Judgement. It was, is and will be applicable for all time and for all people, from the day it was revealed until the Last Day.

... This is nothing but a reminder for all human beings. (Surat al-Muddaththir: 31)

... But it is nothing less than a reminder for all the Worlds. (Surat al-Qalam: 52)

Allah has, in many verses throughout the Qur'an, outlined His attributes, His might and His favours to His creation. He reveals that He has created the universe; that He is free of worldly needs; that He is free of defects; that He is All-Knowing and All-Seeing. This is important for us to gain a better understanding of the One Whom we worship, so that we can be grateful for His bounties and strive further to please Him. In addition, Allah also speaks to us directly, individually and socially, Muslims and non-Muslims, giving reassurance and support, good news and a warning. He tells us that He is our friend and helper and that human beings should call on Him in times of need.

Since Allah is the Creator of all things, He knows what is best for His creation, both as individuals and as a whole. Therefore, He has outlined in the Qur'an the boundaries of His law *(Shariah)* within which we should act. Allah has clearly explained in the Qur'an what is right and what is wrong; what is lawful and what is forbidden:

It is He Who sent down the Book to you from Him: ayats containing clear judgements – they are the core of the book... (Surah Al 'Imran: 7)

The guidance contained in the Qur'an is full of wisdom and can be grasped without difficulty. The commands and prohibitions enjoined in its verses are clear and easily understandable. An individual with sincere intentions whom Allah has guided to the Right Path can understand these without difficulty and can practise them fully in his actions.

However, the Qur'an is much more than a book of rules. Allah has revealed in the Qur'an how to be sound in body and spirit and what to do in times of difficulty and unexpected adversity and He has described various kinds of human character. Allah has revealed verses that give us the knowledge to solve problems in daily life both as individuals and as a community. In other words, the Qur'an contains all the basic knowledge necessary for every moment in the life of a person or a community, no matter how trivial it may seem.

However, it is only those who fear Allah and abide by His commands and prohibitions, and who submit to Him in their heart and choose the next world over this one, who are able to consider the counsel given in the Qur'an. Allah says in the Qur'an:

> **Will they then not meditate on the Qur'an, or are there locks on the hearts? (Surah Muhammad: 24)**

In order to help us carry out the commands of Allah in our daily lives, the Qur'an tells us of past nations and peoples that have denied or disobeyed Allah. We learn of their end and how they were punished, so that we too may learn a lesson from history. This is a grace from Allah for us.

> **That is some of the news of the cities which We relate to you. Some of them are still standing, while others are now just stubble. (Surah Hud: 100)**

These stories of past nations are also a way to prove to unbelievers that the Qur'an is the Word of Allah. The Prophet 🔱 could not have known a great deal of these details of history, since he had not been taught by any scholars, was not able to read or write and had not travelled extensively. Therefore, this proved that he could not have written the Qur'an. Many of the accounts of the past nations have recently been corroborated by historians and archaeologists. [6]

> **There is instruction in their stories for people of intelligence. This is not a narration which has been invented but**

---

6 *See Perished Nations*, Harun Yahya, Ta-Ha Publishers Ltd., 2002

confirmation of all that came before, a clarification of everything, and a guidance and a mercy for people who have iman. (Surah Yusuf: 111)

Commands and prohibitions have been outlined in the Qur'an for us to achieve the best in the Hereafter. In order to motivate us to do more good, Allah describes in detail what we can expect in the Hereafter according to the purity of our *tawhid* and the deeds that we have performed in this life. The Garden is described in great detail, in order to help us strive to achieve it, if Allah wills. Similarly an equally graphic picture of Hellfire is presented in order to deter us from disbelief, ascription of partners to Allah whether openly or inadvertently, doing bad deeds and thus earning the displeasure of Allah.

It is certainly a reminder to you and to your people, and you will be questioned. (Surat az-Zukhruf: 44)

Allah tells us that He has given us the capacity to judge between right and wrong *(furqan)* and it is with this capacity that He invites us to reflect upon His creation.

And among His signs is the creation of the heavens and the earth, and the variations in your languages and your colours; verily in that are signs for those who know. (Surat ar-Rum: 22)

In several verses of the Qur'an, there are references to scientific matters that have recently been advanced by researchers, sometimes working with the aid of advanced technology or abstruse mathematics. At the time when the Qur'an was revealed, it was impossible to discover these matters scientifically, which once more is a serious indication to those who disbelieve that the Qur'an is Allah's word to humanity.

When the Qur'an was revealed in the seventh century CE, the Arabs had innumerable myths about the world. They did not have the technology to investigate the universe and the world of nature, but believed in myths and legends passed down from generation to generation. For example, they believed that the sky was held up by mountains; that the earth was flat and high mountains at the two ends of the earth acted as columns supporting the vault of the heavens. Myths such as these were eradicated with the revelation of the Qur'an:

Allah is He Who raised up the heavens without any support…
(Surat ar-Ra'd: 2)

About this and many other matters, the Qur'an imparted important knowledge about things that were unknown to most people at that time. When the Qur'an was sent down, human beings knew very little about astronomy, physics and biology; it contained important knowledge about many things such as the creation of the universe and human beings, the components of the atmosphere and the balance in nature. Indeed there are facts in the Qur'an which we still do not understand or appreciate because we do not have the capability as yet to grasp them.

Much detailed knowledge about this world and the world to come is explained rationally in the Qur'an. This is the uniqueness of the Qur'an. Although the Qur'an contains much material for those with the requisite intellect, knowledge and scholarship, it does not take high intellect, broad culture or ability for the average person to understand the Qur'an; it is only necessary to have sincerity. The Qur'an has been sent to all humanity, but it is only the way to the Right Path for those who fear Allah and believe in the Last Day:

Those are the Signs of the Wise Book – guidance and mercy for
the good-doers. (Surah Luqman: 2-3)

Mankind! Admonition has come to you from your Lord and also
healing for what is in the breasts and guidance and mercy for
the believers. (Surah Yunus: 57)

Bediuzzaman Said Nursi said that the Qur'an is a guide to the truth for devoted slaves of Allah:

The All-Wise Qur'an is the leader to the aware and the conscious, the
guide of jinn and men [and women], the teacher of those attaining to
perfection, and instructor of those seeking reality. [7]

---

7 Bediuzzaman Said Nursi, *Risale-i Nur Collection*, "The Letters: The Twenty-sixth Letter, The First Topic", http://www.risale-inur.com.tr/rnk/eng/words/15th_word.htm

The Qur'an says that the words of Allah are whole and complete and a person can only reach the truth if he takes the Qur'an and the Sunnah of the Prophet ﷺ as his guides.

> **...We have not omitted anything from the Book... (Surat al-An'am: 38)**

> **Those We have given the Book know it has been sent down from your Lord with truth, so on no account be among the doubters. The Words of your Lord are perfect in truthfulness and justice. No one can change His Words. He is the All-Hearing, the All-Knowing. (Surat al-An'am: 114-115)**

The Protection of the Qur'an

One of the most important aspects of the Qur'an is that it has come down to us without change from the time it was revealed to the Prophet Muhammad ﷺ:

> **It is We Who have sent down the Reminder and We Who will preserve it. (Surat al-Hijr: 9)**

> **No one can change His words... (Surat al-Kahf: 27)**

The Qur'an is not the first revelation from Allah to mankind, as is explained in the Qur'an itself:

> **He has sent down the Book to you with truth, confirming what was there before it. And he sent down the Torah and the Injil, previously, as guidance for mankind... (Surah Al 'Imran: 2-3)**

However, the miracle of the Qur'an is that it is the last revelation of Allah, and it is recited to this day as it was recited 1400 years ago. It will remain unchanged for all time. The previous revealed scriptures were altered from their original states. Over the years, people have made additions, changes or completely excised various portions.

But when a revelation came to the Prophet ﷺ, Allah miraculously enabled him to memorise it. Immediately afterwards, the Prophet ﷺ had the Qur'an written by certain men among the Companions called the 'recorders of revelation'. Thus, the Qur'an was preserved in its written form. During the caliphate of Abu Bakr ❀ the Qur'an was compiled in one volume and it was during the caliphate of 'Uthman ❀ that multiple copies were made and sent to the major cities of Islam.

It is because of this Divine protection that the Qur'an is such a powerful book, with the permission of and by the will of Allah:

> **...And indeed it is a Book of exalted power. No falsehood can approach it from before or behind it: It is sent down by One full of wisdom, worthy of all praise. (Surah Fussilat: 41-42)**

> **If We had sent down this Qur'an onto a mountain, you would have seen it humbled, crushed to pieces out of fear of Allah. We make such examples for people so that hopefully they will reflect. (Surat al-Hashr: 21)**

There are numerous benefits to be gained by reciting it and even more by understanding it, both in this world and in the Hereafter.

> **A light has come to you from Allah and a clear book. By it Allah guides those who follow what pleases Him to the ways of peace. He will bring them from the darkness into the light by His permission and guide them to a straight path. (Surat al-Ma'idah: 15-16)**

> **This is clear insight for mankind and guidance and mercy for people with certainty. (Surah al-Jathiyah: 20)**

> *On the authority of 'Abdullah ibn Mas'ud, it is narrated that the Prophet* ❀ *said: 'The Qur'an is an intercessor, which has been made to intercede, and it is rightfully believed in. Whoever puts it in front of him, it will lead him to Paradise; whoever puts it behind him, it will steer him to Hellfire.' (At-Tabarani)*

Recitation of the Qur'an brings tranquillity to the heart and peace to the soul. It is a guidance and mercy from Allah to all believers.

> **Only in the remembrance of Allah can the heart find peace. (Surah Ra'd: 28)**

> **When the Qur'an is recited listen to it and be quiet so that hopefully you will gain mercy. (Surah al-'Araf: 204)**

5. The Miracle of the Prophet Muhammad's ﷺ Noble Character

The Prophet Muhammad ﷺ was a blessed man and greatly honoured in the sight of Allah. Allah created him to be obedient and made him great in the world; he had the kind of character that made him the most trustworthy of all human beings and he was an example to others in his honesty. He was a noble messenger of Allah whose *taqwa*, excellent character and disposition were exemplary. With his compassion, courtesy, subtle understanding, trust in Allah and patient determination, he is a spiritual guide for all humanity, and an example to us all.

Ibrahim ibn Muhammad, a grandson of Ali ﷺ, had this to say about the Prophet ﷺ:

Whenever Ali ﷺ described the noble features of the Messenger of Allah ﷺ, he used to say: 'He was the most generous and the most truthful. He was the most kind-hearted. Any person who saw him suddenly would become awed. Anyone who came in close contact with him, and knew his excellent character loved him. The one who described him said: "I have not seen anyone like him before him or after him."' (At-Tirmidhi)

In the community where he lived, the Prophet ﷺ was well known as al-Amin (the Trustworthy One); everyone agreed that he was honest and reliable. The Prophet's ﷺ face shed a noble light that convinced everyone who saw it of his honesty. Anyone who listened to the voice of his conscience while speaking with him or joining in a conversation with him understood that he was special; they saw many proofs that he was a prophet. He was intelligent and insightful and, because of the excellence of his character, even unbelievers referred to him to solve misunderstandings that arose among them.

Ibn Sa'd narrated the following account that he received from Ibn 'Asakir concerning the virtue and goodness that the Companions continually witnessed in the Prophet ☙:

> *The Prophet of Allah grew as the best among people in terms of honesty, the most beautiful in character, the most perfect in social relations, the most generous in neighbourliness, the most forward in gentleness and security, the truest spoken, and he who attached greatest importance to courtesy and good manners. He got on well with all. For that reason they called him al-Amin – the truest and most trustworthy.* [8]

Ibn Sa'd related the following from Ibn Hisham:

> *In the time of ignorance before Islam everyone applied to the Prophet of Allah to resolve disputes.* [9]

Ya'qub ibn Sufyan and al-Bayhaqi received the following from Ibn Shihab:

> *When Quraysh rebuilt the Ka'bah they fell to arguing over the laying of the Black Stone. Each tribe wished to lay it. Then they said: 'Whoever comes from that road, let us appoint him to judge between us.' The first to approach was the Prophet Muhammad* ☙*, who was then still a young man. (He was, according to reliable sources, thirty-five.) They appointed him arbiter. He said, 'Bring a ground cloth.' A ground cloth was brought. 'Now put the Stone on it together,' he said. When the Stone was placed on the cloth he said, 'Let the eldest of each tribe come and hold one end of the cloth.' They carried the Stone to its place in that manner. He then went up and installed the Stone he had taken from them. As he grew he attracted the love and respect of all. Because of the fame his honesty*

---

8 As-Suyuti, *Tahdhib al-khasa'is al-nabawiyyah al-kubra* (The Awesome Characteristics of the Prophet [saas]), Iz Publication, Istanbul, 2003, p. 237
9 *Ibid.*, p. 238

won him he was known as al-Amin, the most trustworthy. This was before the revelation had been made to him.[10]

However, after the Qur'an was revealed to the Prophet 鑊, the attitude of the unbelievers changed. They tried their utmost to prevent the spread of Islam and, despite the fact that they saw the Prophet 鑊 was good both in his personal life and character, they conspired to do him personal harm. Allah tells us in the Qur'an of this:

They are surprised that a Warner should come to them from among themselves. The kuffar say, 'This is a lying magician.' (Surah Sâd: 4)

Nonetheless, those who slandered a good and blessed man chosen by Allah were personal witnesses to his merit. With their own eyes they saw Muhammad's 鑊 faithfulness to his promises, his loyalty, justice, honesty, truthfulness, kindness to widows, orphans and those in need, and his generosity towards and interest in others. The excellence of his character and behaviour always caught the attention of people and he was most people's trusted, beloved and respected friend.

According to Islamic sources, there was a man by the name of Nadr ibn al-Harith who slandered the Prophet 鑊. Then, one day he met with the leaders of Quraysh and told them the following about Allah's blessed Messenger 鑊:

Quraysh, I swear that today you have encountered something that has never befallen you before. From early childhood Muhammad 鑊 was your most beloved, the greatest speaker of truth and the one who achieved the greatest respect. When he was older and brought Allah's Book you said he was a magician. I swear that he is not a magician. We have seen many magicians. We have seen how they breathe on knots. You then called him a seer. I swear that neither is he a seer. How many seers have we seen and witnessed their speech? You called him a poet. I swear that he is not a poet. How many poems have we learned, and seen their metre? You

---

10 *Ibid.*, p. 237

called him mad. I swear that he is not mad. Are there any signs of fainting, nonsense or fits in him? Quraysh, think well and decide... [11]

The great Islamic scholar, Imam al-Ghazali, gives an account of the Prophet's ﷺ excellent character. He collected his information from important scholars of hadith such as At-Tirmidhi, At-Tabarani, Imam al-Bukhari, Imam Muslim, Imam Ahmad, Abu Dawud and Ibn Majah:

The Prophet ﷺ *was the most patient of men, the bravest, the best judge, and one who pardoned most. He was the most charitable of men. He did not store up the provision of his family members that Allah was pleased to give him for more than a year. What remained in excess, he used to give in sadaqah. He used to give away in sadaqah to him who begged anything of him, even out of his stored up provision.*

He used to speak the truth even though it was sometimes a cause of trouble to himself and his companions.

He used to accept invitations to weddings, visit the sick and the diseased and attend funerals. He was the most modest without pride and his tongue was most eloquent without lengthiness of speech. His constitution was the most beautiful.

He used even to go to distant places to visit the sick, ... sit with the poor and destitute, eat with them, honour those possessing nobility, advise them to do good deeds and show kindness to relatives. He did not treat anyone harshly and accepted excuses offered to him.

He joked but spoke the truth.

He held innocent sport and play as lawful, played with his wives and held races with them. He did not belittle the poor for their poverty nor show respect to the wealthy for their riches. He used to call people to Allah. [12]

---

11 *Ibid.*, p. 286
12 Imam al-Ghazali, *Ihya Ulum-ud-din* (Revival of the Sciences of the Deen), trans. by Sitki Gulle, Huzur Publishings, Istanbul, 1998, pp. 795-796

It was because of the noble character of the Prophet🏵, his extraordinary determination in the face of adversity and his generous nature that Allah was pleased with him and described his virtues in the Qur'an:

> **You will have a wage which never fails. Indeed you are truly vast in character. (Surat al-Qalam: 3-4)**

> **...this is the word of a noble Messenger. (Surat al-Haqqa: 40)**

It was the combination of Allah's help, His divine revelation and the strength of character of the Prophet🏵 that a whole society came out of the darkness and into the light over a short period of twenty-three years. People who had mistreated their women and children to the point of burying baby daughters alive, who had treated poor people and slaves cruelly, now became compassionate and just in the light of Islam. People who worshipped idols of stone and held numerous myths and superstitions, now believed in the Oneness of Allah.

In order to bring about this radical and lasting change, the Prophet🏵 endured much suffering. He was offered great material rewards by the unbelievers if he would stop preaching the word of Allah, but the Prophet🏵 rejected all such proposals. He was a principled man, only desiring Allah's approval and the good of Islam and the Muslims. He hoped for Allah's help even in the most difficult of circumstances and he believed that He would always allow him and the believers to prevail. Allah rewarded him and the believers by supporting them and protecting them from those who had no faith.

The Miracle of the Prophet 🏵 Being Untaught (*Ummi*)

When the Prophet🏵 received the Qur'an, he could neither read nor write; in other words, he was untaught. This was one of the most important indications that he was a prophet.

Although they knew that the Prophet🏵 was untaught, the

unbelievers did not accept that the Qur'an was revealed to him, and accused him of writing it himself. Yet, those without faith had known the Prophet ﷺ before his prophethood and were well aware that he did not possess the knowledge to do this. Allah says in the Qur'an:

Accordingly We have revealed to you a Ruh by Our command. You had no idea of what the Book was, nor faith. Nonetheless We have made it a Light by which We guide those of Our slaves We will. Truly you are guiding to a Straight Path. (Surat ash-Shura: 52)

Allah has sent down the Book and Wisdom to you and taught you what you did not know before. Allah's favour to you is indeed immense. (Surat an-Nisa': 113)

The Prophet ﷺ conveyed the Qur'an to humanity as a 'revelation from Allah'; he never claimed to be a writer or poet and reminded people that they had known him for years before he became a prophet:

Say: 'Had Allah so wished, I would not have recited it to you nor would He have made it known to you. I lived among you for many years before it came. Will you not use your intellect?' (Surah Yunus: 16)

Despite the fact that he was untaught, the Prophet ﷺ delivered his message very effectively. Allah gave him knowledge by revelation of what was contained in the Tawrah and Injil. When Allah revealed the Qur'an, He gave him knowledge of other revealed books and societies that had passed away. This would have been impossible without Allah's revelation to the Prophet ﷺ. Al-Ghazali expands on the qualities of the Prophet ﷺ:

The character and conduct of the Prophet ﷺ, his actions, his habits, management of affairs, his treatment of the different classes of people, his showing the straight path to them, his wonderful answers to different difficult and subtle questions, his untiring efforts for the good of people, his good guidance regarding the open laws of Shari'ah; all these matters lead one to the conclusion that these were beyond the power of a man without the help of an unseen hand. It is impossible on the part of a hypocrite or a liar. The people testified on seeing his constitution and qualifications that he was a great truthful man sent by Allah.

Allah gave him these qualities though he was untaught and had no education and lived always among illiterate Arabs. Being untaught, an orphan and weak, how did he acquire such good character and conduct, such knowledge about Allah without worldly or other-worldly education? His true and correct knowledge about the earlier prophets, peace be upon them, shows that he is a true messenger of Allah, because he knew these truths by revelations. How could he know what was beyond man unless he received revelation? [13]

All those who knew him, including the unbelievers, were aware that the Prophet ❋ had never sat with learned people to receive an education; and the wisdom in his message could only be a miracle granted by Allah to His messenger. Allah says in the Qur'an:

You never recited any Book before it nor did you write one down with your right hand. If you had, the purveyors of falsehood would have voiced their doubts. (Surat al-'Ankabut: 48)

The *Encyclopaedia of Seerah* tells how the great knowledge that Allah gave to Muhammad ❋ is proof that he was His messenger:

The Prophet Muhammad ❋ was untaught; he could not read or write. Throughout his life the members of the family he grew up in, those close to him and the people of Makkah never saw him touch a book nor hold a pen. Therefore, the Qur'an, the sea of knowledge revealed to him, is a unique miracle. That is because the text contains treasures of information such as the main subject matter of all previous divine scriptures, stories of previous prophets, religions and their beliefs, ancient history, civilisation, culture

---

13 Imam al-Ghazali, *Ihya 'ulum ad-din* (Revival of the Sciences of the Deen), vol. II, English Translation by Fazlul Karim, Islamic Book Services, New Delhi, 2001, p. 252

and economics, politics and moral values. ... The way that, despite being untaught himself, he appeared before the unbelievers with a Book is in any case the greatest proof of his prophethood. [14]

Jewish Scholars Recognise the Prophet ﷺ

Jews and Christians, described in the Qur'an as the 'People of the Book', have certain corruptions in their beliefs and practices; but despite this, they follow a religion that was originally sent down by Allah. The Tawrah and Injil were revealed books of Allah, although they were changed over time. Allah has said that the Qur'an was sent down as the final book to humanity, confirming what was in the previous revealed books. In the following ayat, Allah addresses the Children of Isra'il:

> **Have iman in what I have sent down, confirming what is with you. Do not be the first to reject it and do not sell My Signs for a paltry price. Have taqwa of Me alone. (Surat al-Baqarah: 41)**

The coming of an untaught prophet was foretold in the Tawrah and Injil and so the scholars of these books would have known about the Prophet Muhammad ﷺ and also of the revelation of the Qur'an as the final Word of Allah:

> **It is certainly in the scriptures of the previous peoples. Is it not indeed a Sign for them that the scholars of the tribe of Israel have knowledge of it? (Surat ash-Shu'ara': 196-197)**

In his work *al-Asas fi't-Tafsir*, the interpretive scholar, Imam Sa'id Hawa, explains these verses of the Qur'an as follows:

> *It is certain that the Qur'an existed in earlier books. In other words it is referred to in earlier scriptures, or the senses it contains were transmitted by the prophets of other communities and were present in their books in the manner revealed by Allah, as can be seen in Divine texts.*

> *...Moderate and honest Jewish scholars know that the Tawrah, Psalms*

---

14 Afzalur Rahman, *Encyclopaedia of Seerah: Muhammad (saas)*, Inkilap Publishing, Istanbul, 1996, p. 162

*and Injil contain the contents of the Qur'an, and that every element in it
is the truth from Allah and that this is the last book and the last prophet
of whom the earlier scriptures speak.* [15]

When the Prophet ✺ came, many of the Jewish and Christian scholars
immediately recognised that he was the untaught prophet that had been
foretold in their scriptures. The Prophet ✺, through the revelation of the
Qur'an knew of the contents of the Tawrah and Injil and about the
history of the Bani Isra'il, as typified by the following verse:

**Tribe of Israel! Remember the blessing I conferred on you.
Honour My contract and I will honour your contract. Have
dread of Me alone. Have iman in what I have sent down,
confirming what is with you. Do not be the first to reject it and
do not sell My Signs for a paltry price. Have taqwa of Me alone.
Do not mix up truth with falsehood and knowingly hide the
truth. (Surat al-Baqarah: 40-42)**

When Muhammad ✺ read them these verses, the wise men of the
Israelites recognised him as the Messenger whose coming they were
awaiting. The People of the Book saw that he was the Messenger of
Allah and that he spoke the truth in every respect. In his way of life and
character, he was that blessed Messenger whose coming was foretold in
the Tawrah and Injil. The Qur'an says:

**Those who follow the Messenger, the Unlettered Prophet,
whom they find written down with them in the Torah and the
Gospel, commanding them to do right and forbidding them to
do wrong, making good things halal for them and bad things
haram for them, relieving them of their heavy loads and the
chains which were around them. Those who have iman in him
and honour him and help him, and follow the Light that has**

---

15 Imam Sa'id Hawa, *al-Asas fi't-Tafsir* (The Basics of Qur'anic Commentary), Samil Yayinevi,
Istanbul, 1991, p. 332

been sent down with him, they are the ones who are successful. (Surat al-A'raf: 157)

The Islamic scholar, Omer Nasuhi Bilmen, explains this verse in his commentary of the Qur'an, as follows:

This verse reveals that those possessed of the most distinguished qualities, the best deeds and excellences in this world and the Hereafter, are the followers of the Khatam al-Anbiya (Last Prophet): those who follow the Prophet Muhammad – to whom the Divine Book, in which the knowledge of the past and future are contained, was revealed, though he read nothing from anyone and wrote nothing – achieve the honour of being of his community. He is referred to by name or by his characteristics – in the Tawrah and the Injil. There can be no doubt that he is present in name and in his characteristics in these books. If such were not written in those books would the Prophet Muhammad claim to be [referred to] and thus give grounds for his rejection? He is such a great Prophet that he commands and advises those whom he calls to faith, all humanity, to respect and honour the commands of Allah, to acquire proper belief and morality, and to show affection to creatures (and he forbids the wrong). [16]

The fact that the coming of the Prophet and his qualities were foretold to the People of the Book is another of the miracles associated with him. Those of the People of the Book, who, with faith and common sense, used their intellects to consider the things they saw, have confirmed this evident truth.

---

16 Omer Nasuhi Bilmen, *Ku'ran-i Kerim'in Turkçe Meali* (Tafsir of the Qur'an), vol. 2, Bilmen Basim ve Yayinevi, Istanbul, pp. 1101-1102

6. Some Miracles in the Life of the Prophet Muhammad ﷺ

There were a number of miracles granted to the Prophet ﷺ throughout his life. As mentioned previously, the revelation of the Qur'an and the Qur'an itself are the greatest of these miracles. The excellent character of the Prophet ﷺ, his actions and even his hadith are all miracles. There are a number of other miracles that took place during the life of the Prophet ﷺ that have been related in the Qur'an and the *seerah* (the biography of the Prophet ﷺ). Below is a selection of just some of these miraculous events.

Prophet Muhammad's ﷺ Night Journey and Ascent to Heaven (al-Isra wa'l-Mi'raj)

One of the most remarkable miracles that occurred in the life of the Prophet ﷺ was *al-Isra wa'l-Mi'raj* (The Night Journey and Ascent), which took place about 17 months before the Hijrah. The Night Journey *(Isra')* is described in the first verse of Surat al-Isra':

Glory be to Him Who took His slave on a journey by night from the Masjid al-Haram to the Masjid al-Aqsa, whose surroundings We have blessed, in order to show him some of Our Signs. He is the All-Hearing, the All-Seeing. (Surat al-Isra': 1)

According to hadith, the Prophet ﷺ was sleeping next to the Ka'bah when Jibril appeared to him, mounted him on a white creature in-between a mule and a donkey called the *Buraq* and took him from the Masjid al-Haram to the Masjid al-Aqsa. The Masjid al-Haram is the

41

great mosque in Makkah and the Masjid al-Aqsa is the mosque in Jerusalem (the word *aqsa* means farthest); the distance between these two places is about 1235 kilometres.

It was from the Masjid al-Aqsa that the Prophet ﷺ embarked on the second stage of his journey – the ascent through the heavens *(Mi'raj)* to the *Sidrat al-Muntaha* (Lote-tree of the Final Limit) and, according to hadith, then beyond that into the presence of Allah, exalted is He, and the meeting with Him. Ibn Kathir says that at least twenty-five of the Companions transmitted the story of the Night Journey from the Prophet ﷺ but that this number could have been as many as forty-five. Those accepted as most reliable are the accounts of Anas ibn Malik, Abu Hurayrah, Abu Sa'id al-Khudri, Malik ibn Sa'sa', Abu Dharr al-Ghifari, Abdullah ibn 'Abbas, Abdullah ibn Mas'ud and Umm Hani.

There is much detailed information in the hadith about what the Prophet ﷺ saw during his *Mi'raj*. In a hadith of Muslim narrated by Anas ibn Malik, we learn of the events that transpired during this miraculous journey. As the Prophet ﷺ ascended through the heavens with Jibril, he in turn met the Prophets Adam عليه السلام, 'Isa عليه السلام, Yahya عليه السلام, Yusuf عليه السلام, Idris عليه السلام, Harun عليه السلام, Musa عليه السلام and Ibrahim عليه السلام. Then he reached the *Sidrat al-Muntaha* and received a revelation (Surat al-Baqarah: 285). From there the Prophet ﷺ was taken into the presence of Allah and it was here that he received the command that Muslims should perform salah.

The Qur'an also describes the Prophet's ﷺ ascent to *Sidrat al-Muntaha*:

> **He saw him again another time by the Lote-tree of the Final Limit, beside which is the Garden of Refuge, when that which covered the Lote-tree covered it. His eye did not waver nor did he look away. He saw some of the Greatest Signs of his Lord. (Surat an-Najm: 13-18)**

On his return, the Prophet ﷺ told Quraysh of the events that had taken place the previous night. The unbelievers, and even some of the weaker Muslims, doubted the miracle of the *Mi'raj* and approached Abu

Bakr ⁓ with baseless accusations about the Prophet 🕌. When the unbelievers asked Abu Bakr ⁓ if he believed the story of the Night Journey and if he would continue to believe in the Prophet 🕌, he replied, "If he said it, then I believe him, yes." For his loyalty in this regard, the Prophet 🕌 gave Abu Bakr ⁓ the title *as-Siddiq* (Completely Faithful).

The unbelievers questioned the Prophet 🕌 in order to find out if he was telling the truth. He 🕌 was able to answer their questions fully and there are accounts of this in the hadith:

> *They said: 'Will you describe the Masjid al-Aqsa to us?' Some of them had been there and seen it.*

> *The Prophet 🕌 related: 'I began describing the Mosque. In describing some places I fell into doubt. At this the Mosque was brought and placed in front of the house of 'Iqal or 'Aqil. I looked at it and began describing it.'*

> *After the Prophet's 🕌 address they said: 'As for the description, by Allah, he was correct!' (Imam Ahmad, Musnad)*

> *'I remember being in al-Hijr, and Quraysh were asking me about my Night Journey. They asked me things about Bayt al-Maqdis that I was not sure of... Then Allah raised Bayt al-Maqdis up for me to see, and there was nothing they asked me about but I told them about it.'* [17]

Nevertheless, the unbelievers still refused to believe in the miracle of the ascent and wanted proof. With Allah's help, the Prophet 🕌 was able to give them the proof that they wanted and they were unable to deny this:

> *They said to the Prophet 🕌, 'What is your proof?' The Prophet 🕌 replied: 'I encountered a caravan belonging to Quraysh. It was at such-and-such a place. The caravan was frightened by us, and changed course. There was a black and a white sack on one camel in the caravan, which [camel]*

---

17 Ibn Kathir, *Tafsir of Qur'an with Hadiths*, vol. 9, Istanbul, Cagri Publications, 1996, p. 4623

cried out and then collapsed.' When the caravan returned they asked what had happened, and they described the events just as the Prophet ﷺ *had.* [18]

The Night Journey and Ascent (*Isra' wal Mi'raj*) was a great miracle given to the Prophet ﷺ, which lent much strength to his message. The event itself was a great miracle as was the fact that Allah helped His messenger to answer the doubts of the unbelievers, thus establishing the Prophet ﷺ as a truthful individual.

Allah Split the Moon in Two for the Prophet ﷺ

Another extraordinary miracle granted to the Prophet ﷺ was the splitting of the moon in two as mentioned in the Qur'an:

The Hour has drawn near and the moon has split. (Surat al-Qamar: 1)

The phrase 'and the moon has split' (*wa'nshaqqa al-qamar*) is a verbal clause consisting of the words 'split' and 'moon'. The verb 'split' comes from the basic Arabic root meaning 'to divide' in the sense of 'the appearance of a plant after the earth has been ploughed'. In this sense, 'splitting' means 'to be divided', 'to be cut into pieces', 'to be separated'.

The story of the splitting of the moon is told in the works of the great scholars of hadith such as Imam al-Bukhari, Imam Muslim, at-Tirmidhi, Ahmad ibn Hanbal, Abu Dawud, Al-Hakim, Al-Bayhaqi, and Abu Nu'aym.[19] A selection of these hadith is given below:

Abdullah ibn Mas'ud (said): 'We were along with Allah's Messenger ﷺ *at Mina, when the moon was split in two. One part was behind the mountain and the other one was on this side of the mountain. Allah's Messenger* ﷺ *said to us: "Bear witness to this."' (Muslim)*

'Abdullah ibn Mas'ud reported that the moon was split in two parts

---

18 *Ibid.*, p. 4615
19 Ilyas Celebi, *Itikadi Açidan Uzak ve Yakin Gelecekle Ilgili Haberler* (Faith-Related Prophecies for the Far and Near Future), Istanbul, 1996, p.161

during the lifetime of Allah's Messenger🌞. 'The mountain covered one of its parts and one part of it was above the mountain and Allah's Messenger🌞 said: "Bear witness to this."' (Muslim)

During the lifetime of Allah's Messenger🌞 the moon was split in two; one part remained over the mountain, and the other part went beyond the mountain. On that, Allah's Messenger🌞 said, 'Witness this miracle.' (Al-Bukhari)

It was, in fact, the people of Makkah who had asked the Prophet🌞 for a clear sign from Allah, and the Prophet🌞 had, by the permission of Allah, shown them the splitting of the moon:

The people of Makkah asked Allah's Messenger🌞 to show them signs (miracles) and he showed them the splitting of the moon twice. (Muslim)

Despite the clear and undeniable nature of this miracle, the idolaters of Quraysh still denied and refused to believe. However, because they could not challenge what they had seen, they chose instead to discredit it by calling it witchcraft or magic:

If they see a Sign they turn away, saying 'There is no end to this witchcraft!' They have denied the truth and followed their whims and desires, but everything has its time. (Surat al-Qamar: 2-3)

'Our eyesight is befuddled! Or rather we have been put under a spell!' (Surat al-Hijr: 15)

Bediuzzaman Said Nursi relates that this miracle was witnessed by many of the Companions and he tells us how powerless the idolaters were in the face of this event:

Among his greatest miracles, a certain mutawatir one [transmitted by so many people in each generation as to be impossible of doubt] is the splitting of the moon. This miracle was related through various channels, to the degree of tawatur, and by the foremost among the Companions such as Ibn Mas'ud, Ibn 'Abbas, Ibn 'Umar, 'Ali, Anas and

Hudhayfah ﷺ. *Moreover, the Qur'an also announced this supreme miracle to the whole world:*

The Hour has drawn near and the moon has split. (Surat al-Qamar: 1)

Even the stubborn unbelievers of the time could not deny this verse; all that they said was, 'It is magic.' Thus, even the unbelievers were certain of the splitting of the moon. [20]

Nursi continues by explaining the reason for the subtle nature of this miracle:

Miracles take place in order to prove the claim of prophethood and to convince deniers, but not to force them to believe. This miracle was needed to convince those who had already heard of the prophethood of Muhammad ﷺ. To let it be seen from other parts of the world, or to demonstrate it in an undeniably obvious way, therefore, would have been contrary both to the wisdom of the All-Wise Creator and to the purpose of man's function in the universe, which is to open the way for the mind without disabling the free will. If the All-Wise Creator had, in accordance with the whims of materialist philosophers, left the moon in the same condition for a few hours to show it to the entire world, and if this fact had thereby been recorded by all historians, it would have been treated among other astronomical incidents, without being restricted to the messengership of Muhammad ﷺ and without being considered a proof of his prophethood. Or, it would have been such an obvious miracle that it would have forced minds to believe and deprived them of free will. As a consequence, coal and diamonds (or Abu Jahl and Abu Bakr ﷺ) would have been the same and the purpose of man's function in the universe would have been lost... [21]

---

20 Bediuzzaman Said Nursi, *Risale-i Nur Collection*, "The Letters: The Nineteenth Letter, Seventeenth Sign", http://www.risale-inur.com.tr/rnk/eng/letters/19letter.html
21 *Ibid.*, http://www.risale-inur.com.tr/rnk/eng/letters/19letter.html

Trees Responded to the Prophet ﷺ

There are a number of hadith that report how trees obeyed the Prophet ﷺ and responded to the questions he put to them. For example, a mimosa tree testified to the Oneness of Allah and to the Prophethood of Muhammad ﷺ at the request of the Prophet ﷺ himself:

> *Ibn 'Umar said, 'We were with the Messenger of Allah ﷺ on a journey and a Bedouin came up to him and he asked, "Bedouin, where are you going?" He replied, "To my family." He said, "Do you want something good?" The man asked, "What is it?" The Prophet ﷺ said, "That you testify that there is no god but Allah alone without partner and that Muhammed is His slave and messenger." The Bedouin asked, "Who will testify to what you say?" "This mimosa tree." It advanced from the edge of the river valley, furrowing the earth until it stood before him and he ﷺ asked it to testify three times and it did so and then returned to its place.'*
> *(Ad-Darimi, al-Bayhaqi and al-Bazzar)* [22]

Even the inanimate rocks would greet the Prophet ﷺ as he walked past and testify to his position as the Messenger of Allah:

> *Ali ﷺ, and others, narrated: 'I was strolling with the Prophet ﷺ once on the outskirts of Makkah, I noticed that not a tree or a rock he passed did let him pass without murmuring: Peace be upon you, Messenger of Allah.' (At-Tirmidhi)*

By the permission of Allah, trees moved for the ease and convenience of the Prophet ﷺ. The following hadith is one of many in this regard:

> *Ibn Furak mentioned that the Prophet ﷺ was travelling by night during the Ta'if military expedition and became sleepy. A lote-tree in his way split into two halves for him and he passed between the two halves. They remain with their trunks until this day and are well known.* [23]

---

22 Qadi 'Iyad Ibn Musa al-Yahsubi, *Muhammad Messenger of Allah Ash-Shifa*, trans. Bewley, Madinah Press Inverness, Scotland, 3rd print, 1999, p. 165
23 *Ibid.*, p. 167

There is a well-known story of the Prophet ﷺ leaning against a particular palm-tree while delivering his *khutbah*. When the *minbar* was constructed for him and the palm tree was no longer used, it groaned and wept out of love for the Prophet ﷺ:

> *Jabir ibn 'Abdullah said: 'The mosque was constructed of the trunks of palm-trees with a roof laid on top of them. When the Prophet ﷺ addressed the people, he would lean against one of the trunks. When the minbar was built for him, we heard that trunk make a sound like a camel.' (Al-Bukhari)* [24]

Abundance of Food and Water

Allah bestowed numerous blessings, abundance and fruitfulness on the Prophet ﷺ throughout his life. There was *barakah* in everything that he touched or graced with his presence, by the will of Allah. There are reports in the hadith of abundance of food and water in the presence of the Prophet ﷺ even when there seemed to be an apparent shortage.

On one occasion, there was not enough water for people to perform their wudu' and yet scores of people were able to do so by a miracle granted to the Prophet ﷺ:

> *Anas ibn Malik said, 'I saw the Messenger of Allah ﷺ at the time of the 'Asr prayer. People looked for water for wudu' and could not find any, so the Messenger of Allah ﷺ was brought some wudu' water. He then placed his hand in the vessel and commanded the people to do wudu' from it.' He added, 'I saw the water flowing from his fingers, and everyone, down to the last man, did wudu' from it.' (Muslim and al-Bukhari)* [25]

Jabir ibn 'Abdullah reports in a sahih hadith that on another occasion when there was a shortage of wudu' water at al-Hudaybiyah, the

---

24 *Ibid.*, p. 168
25 *Ibid.*, p. 158

Prophet🌸 dipped his fingers into the water vessel and some 15,000 people were able to perform their wudu' from it. [26]

There are similar reports of water actually flowing from between the fingers of the Prophet🌸:

Ibn Abbas reported: 'On a journey, when the Messenger of Allah🌸 appeared in the morning there was no water left among the troops. Someone said, "Prophet of Allah, the army has no water!"

"Is there any at all, even just a little?"

"Yes!"

A bowl containing a little water was immediately brought. The Prophet🌸 placed his fingers in the mouth of the bowl and opened them up. Water was pouring from the right of his finger, like a fountain. He commanded Bilal to call the people: "[Come to] the blessed water!"' (Ibn Hanbal, al-Bayhaqi, Bazzar, at-Tabarani and Abu Nu'aym) [27]

Ziyad ibn al-Harith as-Suda'i narrated: 'The Prophet was travelling. He stopped just before dawn. He then emerged and said to me: "Brother of [the tribe of] Suda, is there any water?"

"No, except for a very little which would not suffice you," I said.

"Put it in a bowl and bring it to me," he commanded.

I did what he said. He put his hand in the water. I saw that water poured from between his two fingers like springs. He then commanded, "Call those of my companions who need water!" I called to them. Everyone took as much water as he wanted. ...

...We said: "Messenger of Allah! We have a well. There is much water in winter, and we gather around it. But in summer the water withdraws and we disperse to other sources of water around us. We have become

---

26 *Ibid.*, pp. 158-159
27 As-Suyuti, *Tahdhib al-khasa'is al-nabawiyyah al-kubra* (The Awesome Characteristics of the Prophet [saas]), Iz Publication, Istanbul, 2003, p. 536

Muslims. Yet we are surrounded by enemies. Please, pray to our Lord that He make the water in our well more plentiful. Thus we will not have to disperse right and left, but can always be around our well."

At this, he asked them to bring seven stones. He rubbed these in his hands and made a prayer about them. Then he commanded: "Take these stones, and when you reach the well throw them into it one by one and mention the name of Allah!" We did what he told us. And we have not been able afterwards to see the bottom of it [meaning the well].' (Al-Harith ibn Usamah in his Musnad, al-Bayhaqi and Abu Nu'aym) [28]

Another hadith relates that water gushed from a place that the Prophet ※ had struck with his foot:

'Amr ibn Shu'ayb said that one time when he was riding behind the Prophet ※ at Dhu'l-Majaz, Abu Talib said to him, 'I am thirsty and do not have any water with me.' The Prophet got down and struck the earth with his feet and water came forth. He said, 'Drink.' [29]

Similarly, the Companions have also reported that there was never a shortage of food at meals attended by the Prophet ※ and that everyone present was able to leave with his hunger satisfied:

In the hadith of Anas about the Messenger of Allah ※ getting married, he says, 'My mother, Umm Sulaym, prepared "hays" and I put it in a pot and took it to the Messenger of Allah and he said, "Put it down and invite so-and-so and so-and-so for me and whomever you meet." I invited them and did not omit anyone I met until they filled the Suffah (a veranda attached to the Prophet's mosque in Madinah where poor Muslims used to sleep) and the room. The Prophet put it in front of him and dipped three fingers into it. People began to eat and then leave. The vessel remained as it had been to start with. The people numbered seventy-one or seventy-two.' (Muslim and al-Bukhari) [30]

---

28 As-Suyuti, *Tahdhib al-khasa'is al-nabawiyyah al-kubra* (The Awesome Characteristics of the Prophet [saas]), Iz Publication, Istanbul, 2003, p. 535
29 Qadi 'Iyad Ibn Musa al-Yahsubi, *Muhammad Messenger of Allah Ash-Shifa*, p. 161
30 *Ibid.*, pp.163-164

On another occasion, Abu Ayyub had prepared enough food only for the Prophet ﷺ and Abu Bakr ؓ. He reports that the Prophet ﷺ told him, 'Invite thirty of the Ansar nobles.' He invited them and they ate and then left. Then he ﷺ said, 'Invite sixty more,' and the same thing happened. Then he ﷺ said, 'Invite seventy more,' and they ate their fill and still left some. None of them left without becoming a Muslim and giving homage. Abu Ayyub said that, in all, one hundred and eighty men ate from this food. *(At-Tabarani and al-Bayhaqi)* [31]

Abu Hurayrah ؓ reported that on yet another occasion, the Prophet ﷺ told him to invite the people of the Suffah on his behalf. He gathered them and a plate was put before them and they ate what they wished and then left. The food remained as it had been when it was laid out except that there were the marks of the finger in it. [32]

These are just some examples of the physical miracles that Allah granted to the Prophet ﷺ. There was no aspect of the Prophet's life that did not contain miracles. There were extraordinary yet undeniable singular events such as the Ascent into the Heavens and the splitting of the moon, as well as more regularly reported incidents such as the trees greeting the Prophet ﷺ. These miracles served to support the message of Allah; strengthen the resolve of the believers and invite unbelievers to come to faith. However, because Allah has also given human beings free will, not everyone who was a witness to these miracles chose to believe. The Prophet ﷺ never claimed that he had the power to perform these miracles. They were granted to the Prophet ﷺ by Allah. The Prophet ﷺ was a blessed man and there was great barakah in his presence as we have seen with the abundance of food and water. There was also great barakah in his prayers for his people.

---

31 *Ibid.*, p. 162
32 *Ibid.*, p. 162

7. The Efficacy of the Prophet's ﷺ Prayers

Like all the other prophets, the Prophet Muhammad ﷺ had an intimate bond with Allah; he was a sincere slave with deep faith and intense *taqwa*. Allah granted his prayers, which enabled his Companions and others around him to witness various miracles.

There was great *barakah* in the prayers (*du'a*) of the Prophet Muhammad ﷺ and a number of hadith detail these prayers and how they were answered.

The Prophet's ﷺ Prayers for Rain (*istisqaa*) Were Answered by Allah

There is a detailed account in the hadith about the Prophet's ﷺ prayers for the blessing of rain being granted by Allah.

Anas ﷺ narrated: 'A man entered the mosque on Friday while the Prophet ﷺ was addressing the people. The man said: "Messenger of Allah, our wealth has been destroyed and we have no transport to the market place. Supplicate for rain for us." The Prophet raised his hands and said: "O Allah, give us rain. O Allah, give us rain. O Allah, give us rain." By Allah, at that time there were no clouds in the sky and there was no house or building between us and the mountain. From behind the mountain came a cloud looking like a shield. By the time it reached the middle of the sky, it burst and started to rain.' (Al-Bukhari and Muslim)

Anas ibn Malik said, 'A man came to the Messenger of Allah ﷺ and said, "Messenger of Allah, our animals are dying and our camels are too weak to travel, so supplicate Allah." The Messenger of Allah※ *supplicated, and it rained on us from one jumu'ah to the next.' (Malik's Muwatta)*

or *'and it rained from that Friday till the next Friday.' (Al-Bukhari)*

Companions Who Received the Benefit of the Prophet's ※ Prayers

The Prophet ※ was a caring and compassionate person, who always showed great concern for the believers. The Qur'an makes mention of this:

A Messenger has come to you from among yourselves. Your suffering is distressing to him; he is deeply concerned for you; he is gentle and merciful to the mu'minun. (Surat at-Tawbah: 128)

In the hadith, he made many recommendations for their health, security and faith and he approached them with mercy and compassion. He also prayed to Allah about many things on behalf of his Companions. In the Qur'an, Allah says the following about the Prophet's ※ prayers for believers:

… and pray for them. Your prayers bring relief to them. Allah is All-Hearing, All-Knowing. (Surat at-Tawbah: 103)

Thus, we know from the Qur'an that the Companions received ease and peace of mind from the Prophet's ※ prayers. Hadith tell us that when the Prophet ※ prayed for the health and long life of some of his Companions, these prayers were answered. For example, we learn from Ibn Kathir that the prayers of the Prophet ※ made some of the Companions young:

It is also stated that those Companions for whom the Prophet ※ prayed for long lives lived a hundred years. [33]

---

33 Ibn Kathir, *The Virtues and Noble Character of the Prophet Muhammad (saas)*, Istanbul, Celik Yayinevi, 1982, p. 325

He stroked the head of another Companion and prayed, 'Allah make him beautiful, and make that beauty long-lasting,' and that Companion's face remained young and handsome until he died. [34]

The Prophet ﷺ also prayed for their material wealth.

Anas ﷺ narrated: 'The Prophet ﷺ said, "O Allah! Give him (i.e. Anas) property and children and bless him." Thus I am one of the richest among the Ansar and have had numerous children.' (Al-Bukhari and Muslim)

The Prophet of Allah ﷺ said to 'Abd ar-Rahman ibn 'Awf, 'May Allah make you plentiful!' Ibn Sa'd and al-Bayhaqi relate this from another source and add: ''Abd ar-Rahman said, "I have become so wealthy that whichever stone I raise I know I will find gold or silver".' [35]

The Prophet of Allah ﷺ prayed for al-Baraqi. He reached such a level in commerce that he knew that even if he sold soil he would earn from it. [36]

Abu 'Uqayl said that when his grandfather 'Abdullah ibn Hisham ﷺ went to the market to buy wheat he met Ibn az-Zubayr ﷺ and Ibn 'Umar ﷺ, who said: 'Be our partner! Because the Prophet of Allah ﷺ prayed for plenty for you.' At that he shared his wheat with them. Yet, his camel load never grew less due to this abundance. He returned home with it. [37]

---

34 *Ibid.*, pp. 316, 327
35 As-Suyuti, *Tahdhib al-khasa'is al-nabawiyyah al-kubra* (The Awesome Characteristics of the Prophet [saas]), Iz Publication, Istanbul, 2003, p. 851
36 *Ibid.*, p. 854
37 *Ibid.*, p. 856

8. Allah's Miraculous Protection of the Prophet ﷺ

As we have seen, even before he began to expound the Word of Allah, the Prophet ﷺ was known by everyone as *al-Amin*, signifying his trustworthiness. People who lived in his community trusted him implicitly and chose him as arbiter in many of their problems because of his goodness and justice. Since he was intelligent, forward thinking, insightful and meticulous in everything he did, he earned the respect and admiration of all those around him. However, when the Prophet ﷺ began to call people to believe in Allah and to renounce their idols, the attitude of many unbelieving members of his community suddenly changed.

The idol-worshippers reacted to the Prophet's ﷺ call to justice and truth with insults, as the Qur'an mentions:

> **They say, 'You, to whom the Reminder has been sent down, are clearly mad. Why do you not bring angels to us if you are telling the truth?' (Surat al-Hijr: 6-7)**

The Prophet ﷺ was slandered, ridiculed and subjected to many baseless accusations. Even under these circumstances, he calmly continued to spread the teachings of the Qur'an. However, these teachings caused resentment and anger in the idolaters, who benefited from injustice and oppression and feared that if Islam spread they would lose their worldly status, rank and material wealth. Only a small minority of people appreciated what a mercy the Prophet ﷺ was and the wisdom of his teachings. The idol-worshippers did all they could to make life very difficult for the Prophet ﷺ and those who believed. The Muslims were boycotted, and even tortured and killed by the people among whom they lived. It was because of this hostile environment in Makkah that the Prophet 鷺 and his followers were forced to emigrate to Madinah.

Although the Prophet 鷺 and the believers were welcomed by the *Ansar* of Madinah, the Jews of Madinah were less hospitable. It is a testament to the strength of character of the Prophet 鷺 that he never harboured a grudge against those who wished him ill.

However, the most dangerous group of the Prophet's 鷺 enemies in Madinah were the hypocrites. They pretended to believe and spent time with the Prophet 鷺 yet conspired with the unbelievers against him. Given that the Prophet's 鷺 safety was under threat from these various groups of people, it was a great miracle that the Prophet 鷺 was not harmed in any way during his struggle (except for a few broken teeth and wounds he received on the day of Uhud).

In the Qur'an, Allah promised to protect the Prophet 鷺 from other people who wished him harm:

> **Allah will protect you from people. Allah does not guide the**
> **people of the kafirun. (Surat al-Ma'idah: 67)**

Allah's promise was manifested through many miracles. The deniers, idolaters and hypocrites who wished to harm, or even kill, the Prophet 鷺 were unable to do so. Their plots and traps were always foiled. When the Muslims were forced to engage in combat with the unbelievers, Allah always protected the Prophet 鷺 and helped the believers against the apparently stronger and bigger armies of the unbelievers. The result was that the believers became strengthened in their faith and some unbelievers came to Islam. The Prophet 鷺 was able to continue his mission to the end. As the Qur'an says, this was a miracle and there are many stories from the Prophet 鷺 about it in hadith.

The Unbelievers Could not Kill the Prophet 鷺 in Makkah

The unbelievers felt threatened by the spread of Islam as it would compromise their status and wealth. They would gather to discuss how to persuade the Prophet ﷺ to give up his deen or failing that, how to kill him. Allah knew of these plots and plans and outlines them in the Qur'an:

When those who are kafir were plotting against you to imprison you or kill you or expel you: they were plotting and Allah was plotting, but Allah is the Best of Plotters. (Surat an-Anfal: 30)

To start with, the unbelievers offered the Prophet ﷺ worldly benefits, such as wealth and position, as an incentive to give up proclaiming his message. In his *Musnad*, Ibn Abi Shaybah relates the unseemly offer that 'Utbah made to the Prophet ﷺ:

If you want money, we will collect enough money for you so that you will be the richest of us. If you want leadership, we will take you as our leader and never decide on any matter without your approval. If you want a kingdom, we will crown you king over us...

Because the unbelievers valued wealth and power very highly, they thought that the Prophet ﷺ would accept their apparently generous offer:

They wish that you would conciliate them, then they too would be conciliating. (Surat al-Qalam: 9)

However, the Prophet ﷺ was concerned only with winning Allah's approval and desired only His reward and so he refused all their offers.

Having failed to dissuade the Prophet ﷺ with material promises, the unbelievers became angry and began to plot to imprison him. According to Ibn Ishaq, Quraysh met and consulted together about the Prophet ﷺ and told each other: *'You know what degree this individual has come to.'* At this they began discussing. One of them said: *'Let us imprison him somewhere, letting him speak to nobody, and let us keep him there until he dies! Let us give him just enough food to keep him alive!'*

However, the unbelievers could not reach a consensus about this and decided instead to send him into exile. This, too, was regarded as inappropriate, because they felt that Muhammad 襚 would enlist the support of an Arab tribe who would then seek revenge on them. Abu Jahl, an uncle of the Prophet much opposed to Islam, suggested that the best course of action was to kill the Prophet 襚. [38] Such was his hatred for his nephew that he missed no opportunity in threatening the Prophet 襚.

Imam al-Bukhari relates the following in this regard from Ibn 'Abbas:

> *Abu Jahl said, 'If I see Muhammad praying at the Ka'bah, I will tread on his neck.' When the Prophet* 襚 *heard of that, he said, 'If he does so, the angels will snatch him away.' (Al-Bukhari)*

Abu Jahl even went so far as to attempt to carry out his threat and this event is related in the *Seerah*:

> *... Abu Jahl, carrying a very heavy stone, with the intent of fulfilling his oath [to kill him], staggered as he approached the Prophet* 襚 *who was now humbly absorbed in his prayer. Before Abu Jahl was able to get close enough to the Prophet* 襚 *he turned back in deathly fright. His hand had started to wither on the stone whereupon he dropped it and ran as fast as he could. Quraysh rushed towards him and asked what had come over him whereupon he told them he had seen a terrifying camel, with a tremendously large head, enormous shoulders and a fearsome set of teeth that looked as if it was about to devour him if he continued. Later on, the Prophet* 襚 *told his Companions that the camel was none other than Jibril, and if Abu Jahl had persisted he would indeed have seized him.* [39]

Even when the Prophet 襚 was preparing to leave Makkah to go to Madinah, the unbelievers still used this opportunity to hatch a plot to kill him as he left his home. They asked strong young men from all the tribes to assemble outside the Prophet's 襚 house armed with weapons in order to kill him. The plan was that all the men would strike at the same time, so that the responsibility of the Prophet's 襚 death would not fall on

---

38 Afzalur Rahman, *Encyclopaedia of Seerah: Muhammad (saas)*, vol. III, Inkilap Publishing, Istanbul, 1996, p. 104

39 Shaykha Anne Khadeijah Darwish and Shaykh Ahmad Darwish, *The Millennium Biography of Muhammad (saas) The Prophet of Allah*, www.Allah.com

one tribe alone. However, the angel Jibril came to the Prophet 🌸 that night and told him not to sleep in his own bed. The Prophet 🌸 asked Ali to sleep in his own place, knowing that no harm would come to his nephew. The young men had already gathered outside the Prophet's 🌸 house, while he was inside. At the exact moment that the Prophet 🌸 left the house, Allah took away the sight of the men, so that no-one saw him leave. The men waited outside the Prophet's 🌸 house all night and were furious to realise the next morning when Ali came out of the house that their plan to kill the Prophet 🌸 had completely failed. [40]

The Miracles that Allah Performed in the Cave to Protect the Prophet 🌸

While Ali slept in the Prophet's 🌸 bed, the Prophet 🌸 was at the house of his close friend, Abu Bakr 🌸. Together, they left to go to Madinah. The Prophet 🌸 knew that the first place the idolaters would look for him would be on the Madinah road to the north. For this reason he chose to go in the opposite direction. This was the road to Yemen, south of Makkah. After walking about six kilometres along this road they came to the mountain known as Mount Thawr. This was a high mountain that was difficult and dangerous to climb. The Prophet 🌸, with his trusted friend, Abu Bakr 🌸, hid in a cave there for three nights. According to the sources, this cave on Mount Thawr is called 'Athal'. [41]

In the meantime, in order to find the Prophet 🌸, the Quraysh blocked all the roads and stationed armed men to patrol them. Men, both mounted and on foot, combed the area for footprints. They spread across the mountain slopes and valleys. In their search for the Prophet 🌸, the trackers came right up to the mouth of the cave. At that moment,

---

40 According to documents from Islamic and historical sources the Prophet 🌸 left his home in the 14th year after becoming a prophet on the 27th day of the month of Safar (the second Arabic lunar month)
41 Omer Nasuhi Bilmen, *Ku'ran-i Kerim'in Turkçe Meali* (Tafsir of the Qur'an), vol. 3, Bilmen Basim ve Yayinevi, Istanbul, p. 1270

Muhammad put his whole trust in Allah, and, as in other situations throughout his life, here too the Prophet was miraculously delivered by the will of Allah.

When the idolaters finally reached the mouth of the cave in pursuit of the Prophet and Abu Bakr, they saw a spider's web at the entrance and noticed that pigeons had made their nest there and laid eggs. Quraysh took this to mean that no-one could have recently entered the cave and so they turned back. This was a great miracle of Allah, Who caused the spider to weave its web at the cave entrance and quietly placed the pigeons there. Nothing happened to the Prophet or his companion in the cave; and it is surely a miracle that Allah supported him with invisible armies and gave him a sense of security and well being in his heart, as the Qur'an says:

> **If you do not help him, Allah did help him when the kuffar drove him out and there were two of them in the cave. He said to his companion, 'Do not be despondent, Allah is with us.' Then Allah sent down His serenity upon him and reinforced him with troops you could not see. He made the word of the kuffar undermost. It is the word of Allah which is uppermost. (Surat at-Tawbah: 40)**

In the *Tafsir Ibn Kathir*, this miracle is explained as follows:

> *Allah says, **'If you do not help him'**, that is, it does not matter if you did not help the Prophet Muhammad, for Allah helped him as He helped him when, **'the kuffar drove him out and there were two of them'**. This expulsion is a reference to the year when the idolaters intended to kill the Prophet, so he escaped from them, along with his companion. They both concealed themselves in the cave on Thawr for three nights, with the enemy prowling around in great numbers, in fruitless search of them. It was then that Abu Bakr felt afraid lest the disbelievers would see them and harm them. However, the Prophet was certain of Allah's protection and support, and so reassured Abu Bakr.*

On the authority of Anas ﷺ*, Imam Ahmad reported that Abu Bakr as-Siddiq* ﷺ *said: 'I was in the company of the Prophet* ﷺ *in the cave, and on seeing the kuffar, I said, "Messenger of Allah! If one of them (kuffar) should look towards his feet, he would see us under his feet." He* ﷺ *said, "What do you think of two (people), the third of whom is Allah?"' Al-Bukhari and Muslim also reported the same hadith.*

Therefore Allah says, **'then Allah sent down His serenity upon him'** *, that is He sent down His peace, tranquillity and support upon His Messenger* ﷺ*. And* **'reinforced him with troops you could not see'***, that is, the angels. As for the verse,* **'He made the word of the kuffar (deniers) undermost. It is the Word of Allah which is uppermost'** *, Ibn Abbas said: 'The word of the kuffar refers to association of partners with Allah, while the Word of Allah refers to "La ilaha ill'Allah".'* [42]

Allah Supported the Prophet ﷺ and the Believers During Battle

The revelation of the Qur'an to the Prophet ﷺ lasted twenty-three years. For the first thirteen of these years, Muslims lived as a minority among the idolaters of Makkah and suffered great oppression. Many Muslims were physically tortured, some were killed; others had their houses and possessions plundered and were constantly subjected to insults and threats. In spite of this, Muslims lived without resorting to violence, always trying to make peace with the idolaters. Finally, when the pressure from the idolaters became unbearable, the Muslims moved to the city of Yathrib (later called Madinah) and with the inhabitants, both Arabs and Jews, set up their own society. Allah then gave the Muslims the permission to defend themselves if they were under threat from the unbelievers. When the unbelievers waged war on the Muslims,

---

42 *Tafsir Ibn Kathir*, abridged by Sheikh Muhammad Nasib Ar-Rafa'i, Al-Firdous Ltd., London: 2002, pp.145-146; hadith from Musnad Ahmad, Sahih al-Bukhari: 3653 and Sahih Muslim: 2381

Allah assisted the Prophet 變 with many psychological, spiritual and physical miracles in order to help him defend himself and spread Islam.

The Prophet 變 was a brave and heroic man who fought in open battle and came face to face with the enemy personally. Although he fought in the first rank, he was not killed and, by a miracle of Allah, returned from battle unharmed. Ibn Hanbal, At-Tabarani and Abu Nu'aym relate the following concerning this miracle from Abu Jad'an 變:

> *I saw the Prophet 變. A man was brought before him. 'This man wanted to kill you,' they said. At this the Prophet of Allah said, 'Do not fear! Do not fear! Even had you wished, Allah would not have let you trouble me'.* [43]

Despite knowing that he was the target of the idolaters and hypocrites, the Prophet 變 always ensured that the believers were safe. The Prophet 變 himself knew that he was under Allah's protection on the battlefield and placed himself in His hands, fearing no-one but Him.

The most notable battle in which Allah assisted the Prophet 變 and the believers was the Battle of Badr, which was fought in Ramadan of the second year after the Hijrah. Here Allah assisted the believers with psychological, spiritual and physical miracles starting from even before the fighting had begun.

> **Allah helped you at Badr when you were weak so have taqwa of Allah, so that hopefully you will be thankful. (Surah Al 'Imran: 123)**

Before the two sides actually engaged in combat, both the unbelievers and the believers saw each other's armies as smaller than they actually were. This is described in the Qur'an:

> **Remember when Allah showed them to you in your dream as only a few. If He had shown you them as many, you would have lost heart and quarrelled about the matter; but Allah saved you.**

---

43 As-Suyuti, *Tahdhib al-khasa'is al-nabawiyyah al-kubra* (The Awesome Characteristics of the Prophet [saas]), Iz Publication, Istanbul, 2003, p. 316

He knows what your hearts contain. Remember when Allah made you see them as few when you met them, and also made you seem few in their eyes. This was so that Allah could settle a matter whose result was preordained. All matters return to Allah. (Surat al-Anfal: 43-44)

There was great wisdom behind this miracle of Allah's. When the Muslims saw that the idolaters' army was less numerous than it actually was, it gave them strength and improved their morale. And when the unbelievers saw the Muslim army, already less numerous than theirs, as even smaller, they became careless and were led to think that they would easily be victorious. Ibn Kathir interprets this verse as follows:

*Allah's verse, **'And when you met (the army of the disbelievers), He showed them to you as few in your eyes'**, shows His mercy and kindness towards His believing slaves. He made the Muslims see the idolaters of Quraysh as few in their eyes, in order to encourage them to attack the disbelievers. Abu Ishaq as-Sabi'i narrated that Abdullah Ibn Mas'ud* ﷺ *said: 'Allah showed the Qurayshi army to us as few in our eyes, so much so that I asked a man who was by my side: "They are seventy, aren't they?" and he said: "No, they are a hundred." We then took a man from the Qurayshi army and asked him about their number. He said: "We were one thousand fighters".' ... Allah had excited the state of enmity between the Muslims and the disbelievers, and made each party appear less in the eyes of the other party, so that they would not fear the battle.* [44]

The battle of Badr was a significant milestone in the history of Islam. The Muslims should have been anxious and fearful the night before the battle, tossing in their restless sleep. However, that night they slept soundly and restfully, so that they awoke refreshed and calm. This was also a miracle of Allah:

---

44 Ibn Kathir, *Tafsir al-Qur'an al-'Adhim*, Cagri Yayinlari, Istanbul, 1991, p. 3318

And when He overcame you with sleep, making you feel secure... (Surat al-Anfal: 11)

Also that night Allah sent down rain upon the Muslims. Again there was great wisdom behind this as explained in the Qur'an:

... and sent you down water from heaven to purify you and remove the taint of Shaytan from you, and to fortify your hearts and make your feet firm. (Surat al-Anfal: 11)

The light rain refreshed the Muslims, providing them with water for drinking and for wudu'. The place where the Muslim army encamped was sandy, and so was difficult to walk on as their feet sunk into the ground. The rainwater helped to solidify the ground, making it easier for the Muslims to walk on and 'made their feet firm'. Thus, even before the battle had commenced, the morale of the Muslims was high and their hearts were tranquil.

Once the battle actually commenced, the Prophet ﷺ supplicated to Allah to help him and the Muslims. Allah responded immediately to the plea of the Prophet ﷺ by sending down large numbers of angels to swell the numbers of the Muslims and to assist in the fighting:

Remember when you called on your Lord for help and He responded to you: 'I will reinforce you with a thousand angels riding rank after rank.' Allah only did this to give you good news and that so your hearts would be at rest. Victory comes from no one but Allah. Allah is Almighty, All-Wise. (Surat al-Anfal: 9-10)

In his commentary, as-Sabuni describes the assistance of the angels as follows:

By saying that He would assist with 'a thousand angels riding rank after rank', Allah revealed that He had heeded his prayer. Commentators say that according to the hadith, Jibril brought down five hundred angels and fought with them on the army's right wing. Mika'il also brought down five hundred angels. They fought on the army's left wing. *Apart from Badr, it has not been possible to determine which battles the angels fought in. In other battles, angels descended to make the number of Muslims look greater, but they did not fight.*

Omer Nasuhi Bilmen, further elaborates:

The Prophet ﷺ prayed in the words: 'Lord! Grant me the victory You promised', and fell into a light slumber, and immediately awoke smiling. He addressed Abu Bakr ﷺ, who was by his side: 'Glad tidings, Abu Bakr! Jibril and a great number of the angels have come to our assistance,' he ﷺ said. He ﷺ then donned his armour and left the tent. A number of Muslim warriors were concerned at the numbers of the more numerous enemy army who would take part in the fighting. At this the glad tidings were imparted that help would come to the Muslims from the presence of Allah by means of angels. According to the account, at that moment a powerful wind blew up, and nobody could see anything. This was a sign that Jibril and a great number of the angels had come to the battlefield. Those angels were riding white horses, and appeared in the guise of white and yellow human beings, and physically participated in the battle of Badr.

During the battle of Badr, first one thousand, then two thousand, and then three thousand angels came to assist the Muslims, their numbers finally reaching five thousand. [45]

The effect of supporting the believers with angels was two-fold: on the one hand, this helped the Muslims, but it also instilled terror in the hearts of the enemy. Ibn Kathir includes this in his commentary:

Abu Hurayrah ﷺ reported that the Prophet ﷺ said: 'I have been helped by terror (instilled in the hearts of my enemies) and I have been given concise comprehensive words.' (Muslim) [46]

---

45 Omer Nasuhi Bilmen, *Ku'ran-i Kerim'in Turkce Meali Alisi ve Tefsiri* (Tafsir of the Noble Qur'an), vol. 1, Bilmen Publishings, Istanbul, p. 451
46 Ibn Kathir, *Tafsir of Qur'an with Hadiths*, vol. 7, Istanbul, Cagri Publications, 1993, p. 3447

During the Battle of Badr, the Qur'an explains how, having seen the Muslims as few at another point, the unbelievers saw more people in the Muslim army than there actually were:

There was a sign for you in the two parties which met face to face, one party fighting in the Way of Allah and the other kafirun. They saw them as twice their number with their own eyes. Allah reinforces with His help whoever He wills. There is instruction in that for people of insight. (Surah Al 'Imran: 13)

The unbelievers saw twice as many Muslims as their own numbers, by a miracle of Allah, and this caused them to be afraid and to panic. This was another way in which Allah helped the Muslims and humiliated the unbelievers.

In other battles, angels were also sent to swell the numbers of believers so that the Muslim army would appear more numerous and powerful. The following verse refers to the battle of Hunayn, fought in the eighth year of the Hijrah:

Then Allah sent down His serenity on His Messenger and on the muminun, and sent down troops you could not see, and punished those who were kafir. That is how the kuffar are repaid. (Surat at-Tawbah: 26)

In the Prophet's ﷺ time, one of the miracles that Muslims experienced was that they were not afraid and hesitant when armies were ranged against them. The Qur'an tells us that unbelievers collected many powerful men to do them harm and tried to oppress the Muslims who were fewer in number. In this situation, the Muslims turned sincerely to Allah and put their trust in Him. Because of His protection and support they were abundantly blessed and had a safe return. For example, another miracle that Allah gave the Muslims in battle was the strength and steadfastness to conquer numerous fighters:

O Prophet! Spur on the muminun to fight. If there are twenty of you who are steadfast, they will overcome two hundred; and if there are a hundred of you, they will overcome a thousand of

those who are kafir, because they are people who do not understand. Now Allah has made it lighter on you, knowing there is weakness in you. If there are a hundred of you who are steadfast, they will overcome two hundred; and if there are a thousand of you, they will overcome two thousand with Allah's permission. Allah is with the steadfast. (Surat al-Anfal: 65-66)

A Qur'anic commentary summarises the reasons that Allah provided such powerful support to the Muslims – the fact that they had *taqwa* (fear of Allah) and *sabr* (patience):

> *After Almighty Allah had forbidden us to take intimates of those not of ourselves and declared the reasons why, He promised that He would foil all the traps and snares of the unbelievers so long as we had taqwa and were patient. He showed two situations when He acted as the believing slaves' Guardian, one on the day of Uhud and the other on the day of Badr. On these two days Allah foiled the traps and snares of their enemy on account of the believers' patience and taqwa. The proof that these two incidents have been given as examples of how Allah acted as the believers' Guardian and foiled the snares and ruses of their enemies, because of their steadfastness and taqwa, lies in the fact that steadfastness and taqwa are named in the preceding verse:* **'But if you are steadfast and have taqwa, their scheming will not harm you in any way.'** [47]

For their *taqwa* and *sabr*, the Muslims were rewarded with peace of mind, and spiritual and material well-being. In the Qur'an, Allah tells of the miraculous situation that the Muslims were in:

Those to whom people said, 'The people have gathered against you, so fear them.' But that merely increased their iman and they said, 'Allah is enough for us and the Best of Guardians.' So they returned with blessings and bounty from Allah and no evil

---

47 Sa'id Hawa, *al-Asas fi't-tafsir* (The Basics of Qur'anic Commentary), Samil Yayinevi, Istanbul: 1991, vol. 2, p. 444

touched them. They pursued the pleasure of Allah. Allah's favour is indeed immense. (Surah Al 'Imran: 173-174)

In spite of the fact that the idolaters had all the necessary means at their disposal to put their plots into operation, they were still unsuccessful. This was because the Prophet was a blessed person who acted under Allah's protection. Allah decreed that miraculously they could do no harm to the Prophet:

... their scheming will not harm you in any way. Allah encompasses what they do. (Surah Al 'Imran: 120)

In other verses Allah also promised that no-one would do any physical or spiritual harm to the Prophet:

Were it not for Allah's favour to you and His mercy, a group of them would almost have managed to mislead you. But they mislead no one but themselves and do not harm you in any way. Allah has sent down the Book and Wisdom to you and taught you what you did not know before. Allah's favour to you is indeed immense. (Surat an-Nisa': 113)

They are people who listen to lies and consume ill-gotten gains. If they come to you, you can either judge between them or turn away from them. If you turn away from them, they cannot harm you in any way. But if you do judge, judge between them justly. Allah loves the just. (Surat al-Ma'idah: 42)

9. The Knowledge of the Unseen Given to Our Prophet ﷺ

Only Allah has full knowledge of the Unseen. He knows every detail about the past, present and future. Allah created time and taught this concept to human beings. Allah exists apart from and beyond time. Allah knows and controls everything that happens in the universe. He knows the secret of everything. However, He may choose to impart some of this knowledge to His chosen messengers, to the extent that He wills:

He is the Knower of the Unseen, and does not divulge His Unseen to anyone – except a Messenger with whom He is well pleased, and then He posts sentinels before him and behind him. (Surat al-Jinn: 26-27)

According to the Qur'an, the prophets Yusuf عليه السلام, 'Isa عليه السلام and Muhammad ﷺ were all chosen messengers of Allah who were given some knowledge of the Unseen. Allah revealed many secret matters to the Prophet ﷺ; he knew of past occurrences that no-one else could have known about and also of many events that would happen in the future:

This is news of the Unseen which We reveal to you. (Surah Yusuf: 102)

This knowledge of the Unseen was not an innate ability of the Prophet ﷺ. It was a miracle that was bestowed on him by Allah. He communicated the knowledge of the Unseen to the extent that Allah willed. Throughout his life, the Prophet ﷺ often told people things that could only be known from Allah's revelation and this was a sign that he was indeed a prophet. However, despite this knowledge, obedient to ayat such as the following, the Prophet ✺ remained most humble and submissive:

> **Say: 'I possess no power to help or harm myself, except as Allah wills. If I had had knowledge of the Unseen, I would have sought to gain much good and no evil would have touched me. I am only a warner and a bringer of good news to people who have iman.' (Surat al-A'raf: 188)**

The Prophet ✺ received this unique knowledge from both the Qur'an and also from other Divine revelations given to him. Some of this knowledge was concerning events of the immediate future, such as impending victory in battle; some knowledge concerned events that would take place some years after his death, such as the martyrdom of some of his Companions; while other special knowledge such as the signs of the Last Day are still being witnessed 1400 years after they were first announced. Al-Bukhari, Muslim, Abu Dawud, At-Tirmidhi, An-Nasa'i, Ibn Majah and others agree on the truth of the knowledge of the Unseen related in the stories about the Prophet ✺ in hadith.

The Prophet ✺ Knew of Events that No-One Else Knew About

The Prophet ✺ sometimes knew of events and occurrences that no-one else could possibly know of. This is because Allah revealed this secret knowledge to him. On one occasion, Allah tells us in the Qur'an about a secret that the Prophet ✺ told to one of his wives. However, she told the secret to someone else. Allah told the Prophet ✺ about this. When the Prophet ✺ told his wife that he knew what she had done, she asked him who had told him. Then the Prophet ✺ told her that Allah had informed him. Allah tells us of this event in the Qur'an:

> **The Prophet confided a certain matter to one of his wives, then when she divulged it Allah disclosed that to him, and he communicated part of it and withheld part of it. When he told**

her of it, she said, 'Who told you of this?' He said, 'The All-Knowing and All-Aware informed me of it.' (Surat at-Tahrim: 3)

On another occasion, after the battle of Badr, one of the prisoners taken by the Muslims was Abbas, the Prophet's uncle, who was at that time an unbeliever. When the Prophet ﷺ asked him to pay ransom to the Muslims, his uncle told him that he was unable to do so as he had no money. The Prophet ﷺ then asked his uncle what had happened to the money that Abbas had told his wife, Umm al-Fadl, to keep for him when he had departed from Makkah for the battle.

Abbas asked the Prophet ﷺ how he knew about this fact when it had happened during the night and no-one else was present. The Prophet ﷺ replied that Allah had revealed this fact to him. At that point, Abbas realised that Muhammad ﷺ was the true messenger of Allah and whole-heartedly accepted Islam. (Musnad Ahmad, Muslim and Tafsir Ibn Kathir)

Allah also informed the Prophet ﷺ, through Qur'anic revelations, about the hidden side of some people and their innermost thoughts and actions. He revealed the lies of the hypocrites and their true intentions hidden behind their false words. In this way the Prophet ﷺ was able to ascertain who was a true Muslim and who a hypocrite and thus who he was able to depend upon. This was truly a great support and protection from Allah to the Prophet ﷺ, who was a target for the hypocrites. Allah also informed the Prophet ﷺ how he was to act and what he was to say.

Then He sent down to you, after the distress, security, restful sleep overtaking a group of you, whereas another group became prey to anxious thoughts, thinking other than the truth about Allah – thoughts belonging to the Time of Ignorance – saying, 'Do we have any say in the affair at all?' Say, 'The affair belongs entirely to Allah.' They are concealing things inside themselves which they do not disclose to you, saying, 'If we had only had a say in the affair, none of us would have been killed here in this place.' Say, 'Even if you had been inside your homes, those people

for whom killing was decreed would have gone out to their place of death.' So that Allah might test what is in your breasts and purge what is in your hearts. **Allah knows the contents of your hearts. (Surah Al 'Imran: 154)**

They have the word, 'Obedience!' on their tongues but when they leave your presence, a group of them spend the night plotting to do other than what you say. Allah is recording their nocturnal plotting. **So let them be and put your trust in Allah. Allah suffices as a Guardian. (Surat an-Nisa': 81)**

Those Arabs who remained behind will say to you, 'Our wealth and families kept us occupied, so ask forgiveness for us.' *They say with their tongues what is not in their hearts. Say: 'Who can control Allah for you in any way whether He wants harm for you or wants benefit for you?'* **Allah is aware of what you do. (Surat al-Fath: 11)**

As for those who have set up a mosque, causing harm and out of kufr, to create division between the muminun, and in readiness for those who previously made war on Allah and His Messenger, they will swear, 'We only desired the best.' But Allah bears witness that they are truly liars. Do not ever stand in it. A mosque founded on taqwa from the first day has a greater right for you to stand in it. In it there are men who love to purify themselves. Allah loves those who purify themselves. (Surat at-Tawbah: 107-108)

The Prophet ﷺ Gave Answers Before People Asked the Questions

According to hadith, the Prophet ﷺ was able to answer questions even before they were asked; know who was about to visit his home or enter a room before they did so and even know the reason why someone was late. [48] There are many examples of these miracles in the hadith. In one hadith, the Prophet 🌺 gives an answer to a question that Abu Sufyan ibn al-Harith 🌺 had been pondering:

Abu Sufyan would sit in a corner of the mosque. One day the Prophet 🌺 left his house, wrapped up in his clothing. From where he was sitting Abu Sufyan said, 'I wonder how he was victorious.' The Prophet 🌺 approached Abu Sufyan and struck him on the back with his hand, saying 'I defeated you with the help of Allah.' Abu Sufyan said, 'I bear witness that you are the Prophet of Allah.' (Ibn al-Harith; Ibn Hajar al-'Asqalani, al-Matalib al-Aliyah)

There is a hadith about Wabisah ibn Masad 🌺 in which there is an example of how the Prophet 🌺 could understand the question a person was formulating in his mind and answer it:

Wabisah ibn Ma'bad 🌺 said, 'I came to the Messenger of Allah 🌺 and he said, "You have come to ask about devoutness (birr)?" I said, "Yes!" He said, "Ask your heart for a judgement. Devoutness is that towards which the self is tranquil and towards which the heart is tranquil. Impiety (ithm) is that which becomes agitated in the self and it goes agitatedly to and fro in the breast even though people repeatedly give you a judgement [as to a matter's permissibility]".' (A good hadith narrated in the two Musnads of the Imams Ahmad ibn Hanbal and ad-Darimi with a good isnad.)

Another example of how the Prophet 🌺 knew the thoughts and intentions of a person can be seen in the hadith about how Abu'd-Darda 🌺 became a Muslim:

Abu'd-Darda was worshipping an idol. Abdullah ibn Rawahah and Abu Salamah went and broke that idol. When Abu'd-Darda came and saw the idol in that state he could not refrain from saying [to it], 'Aren't you ashamed, could you not have defended yourself?' Later he came to the

---

48 As-Suyuti, *Tahdhib al-khasa'is al-nabawiyyah al-kubra* (The Awesome Characteristics of the Prophet [saas]), Iz Publication, Istanbul, 2003, pp. 688-689

Prophet 🕌. *Ibn Rawahah saw him on the way and said, 'This is Abu'd-Darda. He must have come to look for us!' The Prophet of Allah* 🕌 *said, 'No! He is coming to become a Muslim. My Lord promised that Abu'd-Darda would become a Muslim.'* [49]

The Prophet 🕌 Foretold His Own Death to His Companions

It was a miracle of the Prophet Muhammad 🕌 that Allah granted him the ability to foretell his own death and that of some of his close companions. In the hadith, the Prophet 🕌 said that he would be the first among the Companions to die:

The Prophet of Allah 🕌 *looked at us and said: 'You suggest that I shall be the last to die. Be warned, I shall die before all of you! You will die after me.'* [50]

Narrated 'Uqbah ibn 'Amir 🕌: *The Prophet* 🕌 *went out and offered the funeral prayer for the martyrs of the (battle of) Uhud and then ascended the minbar and said, 'I will precede you and I am a witness against you, and – by Allah! – I am at this moment gazing upon my pond. And I have been given the keys of the treasuries of the earth' – or 'the treasuries of the earth' – 'And – by Allah! – I do not fear that you will become idolaters after me, but I fear that you will compete for them [the treasuries].'* (Al-Bukhari)

Abu Muwyahibah narrated: The Messenger of Allah 🕌 *called for me in the middle of the night and said to me: 'Abu Muwayhibah, I have been ordered to pray for forgiveness for the people of Baqi' [graveyard], so come with me.' So I departed with him, and when he* 🕌 *stood among them, he said, 'Peace be upon you, dwellers of the graves. May the situation you are in be more comfortable than the situation people are in,*

---

49 *Ibid.*, p. 690
50 *Ibid.*, p. 1115

for tribulations have approached like dark patches of night, one following another, and each one is worse than the one before it.' Then he drew near to me, and said: 'Abu Muwayhibah, I have been given the keys to the treasures of the world and to lasting life in it, followed by the Garden, and was given a choice between this and the meeting with my Lord and the Garden, so I chose the meeting with my Lord and the Garden.' (At-Tabari, Ahmad, Ibn Sa'd, al-Baghawi and Ibn Mandah)

The Prophet ﷺ gave many details about his approaching death, even announcing on which day and in which city he would depart from this world:

… I was born on Monday. The revelation came on Monday. I migrated on Monday and shall die on Monday. [51]

Ibn Abbas ﷺ *narrated: 'The Prophet* ﷺ *was born on a Monday, he became a prophet on Monday, he migrated from Makkah on a Monday and entered Madinah on a Monday. Makkah was opened [to Islam] on a Monday and he died on a Monday.'* (Ibn Hanbal and al-Bayhaqi) [52]

The place to which I migrated and where I shall lie – where I shall be buried when I die – is Madinah! [53]

Madinah is where I emigrated. I shall die there and there be raised up! [54]

The Prophet ﷺ Foretold the Martyrdom of Some of His Companions

As a miracle from Allah, just as he had predicted his own death, the Prophet ﷺ announced the death of some of his Companions long before they died. In these hadith there are many details about the deaths of the Companions. He said that some Companions would be martyred and he revealed the kind of place where they would die.

---

51 *Ibid.*, p. 1120
52 *Ibid.*, p. 1120
53 *Ibid.*, p. 1120
54 *Ibid.*, p. 1121

The Prophet ﷺ Foretold the Martyrdom of Umar ☜

Narrated Anas bin Malik: The Prophet once climbed the mountain of Uhud with Abu Bakr, 'Umar and 'Uthman. The mountain shook with them. The Prophet said (to the mountain), 'Be firm, Uhud! For on you there are no more than a Prophet, a Siddiq and two martyrs.' (Al-Bukhari)

The Prophet ﷺ Foretold the Martyrdom of Uthman ☜

Ibn 'Adi and Ibn 'Asakir narrated from Anas who said: 'The Messenger of Allah ﷺ said: "Uthman! You will be given the caliphate after me but the hypocrites will want you to renounce it. Do not renounce it but fast on that day so that you break your fast with me".' (Narrated from Anas by Ibn 'Asakir in Tarikh Dimashq)

At-Tabarani and al-Bayhaqi narrated from Zayd ibn Arqam ☜ who said: 'The Prophet ﷺ sent me out, saying, "Go and see Abu Bakr. You will find him sitting inside his house wrapped up in his cloth with his legs drawn up. Give him the glad tidings of the Garden. Then go to the mountain until you find 'Umar riding a donkey and his tall frame looming in the distance. Give him the glad tidings of the Garden. Then go to 'Uthman, whom you will find in the market selling and buying, and give him the glad tidings of the Garden after a harrowing ordeal." I went and found them as the Messenger of Allah ﷺ had said, and I told them.' (Zayd ibn Arqam narrated it and it is transmitted by at-Tabarani in al-Awsat, al-Bayhaqi in Dala'il an-nubuwwah, and adh-Dhahabi in the Siyar)

At-Tabarani narrated from Zayd ibn Thabit who said that he heard the Prophet ﷺ say: ''Uthman passed by me while one of the angels was with me and the latter said, "This is a martyr, whose people will kill him. We are shy of him".' (Zayd ibn Thabit narrated it and it is transmitted by at-Tabarani in al-Kabir, 5:159)

The Prophet ﷺ Foretold the Martyrdom of 'Ali ؓ

Al-Hakim - who declared it sound - and Abu Nu'aym narrated from 'Ammar ibn Yasir ؓ that the Prophet ﷺ said to 'Ali ؓ: 'The most grievous of all people is he that shall strike you here' - indicating his temple - 'until blood soaks this' - indicating his beard. (Ahmad in his Musnad, an-Nasa'i in as-Sunan al-Kubra, Abu Nu'aym's Dala'il an-Nubuwwah, and al-Hakim)

At-Tabarani and Abu Nu'aym narrated from Jabir ibn Samurah who said, 'The Messenger of Allah ﷺ said to 'Ali: "You will be given leadership and caliphate; and truly, this will be dyed red with this," meaning his beard with [the blood from] his head.' (At-Tabarani in al-Kabir and al-Awsat)

Al-Hakim narrated from Anas who said: 'I went in with the Prophet ﷺ to see 'Ali who lay sick while Abu Bakr and 'Umar were visiting him. One of them said to the other, "I do not think that he will survive," whereupon the Messenger of Allah ﷺ said: "In truth, he will only die murdered".' (Al-Hakim)

The Prophet ﷺ Foretold the Martyrdom of Husayn ؓ

Ibn Rahwayh, al-Bayhaqi, and Abu Nu'aym narrated from Umm Salamah ؓ, 'The Messenger of Allah ﷺ lay down one day and woke up, holding a handful of red earth in his hand and turning it this way and that. I said: "What is this earth, Messenger of Allah?" He replied: "Jibril informed me that this one - meaning Husayn - would be killed in the land of Iraq, and this is his resting-ground".' (Narrated from Umm Salamah by Ibn Abi 'Asim in al-Ahad wa al-Mathani, at-Tabarani in al-Kabir, and al-Hakim)

Ibn as-Sakan, al-Baghawi, and Abu Nu'aym narrated from Anas ibn al-Harith who said, 'I heard the Messenger of Allah say: "Truly this son of mine" - meaning Husayn – "will be killed in a land called Karbala. Whoever among you is present then, help him!" Hence, Anas ibn al-Harith went to Karbala' and was killed there with Husayn.' (Narrated from Suhaym, from Anas ibn Malik by Abu Nu'aym in the Dala'il and al-Baghawi and Ibn as-Sakan in their Companion-compendiums. Cf. Ibn Hajar, Isabah; al-Bukhari, al-Tarikh al-Kabir; al-Isti'ab; al-Khasa'is al-Kubra)

These predictions about the martyrdoms of Umar, Uthman, Ali and Husayn subsequently came true and, after the Prophet many sincere Muslims who took upon themselves great responsibility for the spread of Islam also died as martyrs.

There are also a great many Qur'anic ayat and hadith that tell of the victory of certain armies and their conquest of various regions several years before these events came to pass:

The Victory of the Byzantines

One of the predictions in the Qur'an about the future is found at the beginning of Surat ar-Rum. In this verse, Allah says that the Byzantine Empire suffered a defeat but that it would soon be victorious again:

Alif, Lam, Mim. The Romans have been defeated in the land nearby, but after their defeat they will themselves be victorious in a few years' time. The affair is Allah's from beginning to end. On that day, the muminun will rejoice. (Surat ar-Rum: 1-4)

The phrase *'in a few years' time'* means between three to nine years.

In 613 the Zoroastrian Persians had defeated the Christian Byzantines at Antioch and went on to be victorious over Damascus, Cilicia, Tarsus, Armenia and Jerusalem. The loss of Jerusalem in 614 and the destruction of the Church of the Holy Sepulchre was a particularly hard blow for the Byzantines. [55] These Qur'anic verses, announcing the victory of the Byzantines, were sent down about seven years later in 620CE.

At this time, there were numerous threats to the Byzantines, not only from the Persians but also from the Avars, Slavs and Lombards. The Avars had come to the outskirts of Constantinople. In order to meet the cost of the army, the Byzantine emperor Heraclius had the gold, silver and other adornments of the churches melted down into coins. Not content with this, he even had bronze statues melted down and the metal used to make coins. Many governors rebelled against Heraclius and it came to the point that the empire was about to be torn apart.

The situation was so dire that it was expected that the Byzantine Empire would collapse and the Arab idolaters were confident that the Qur'an's prediction would never come true.

However, in 622, Heraclius invaded Armenia and defeated the Persians in a number of battles. [56] In December 627, there was a huge battle between the Byzantines and the Persians near the ruins of Nineveh fifty kilometres east of the River Tigris near what would later be Baghdad. Here the Byzantines defeated the Persians. Some months later the Persians were forced to sign a treaty returning occupied lands to the Byzantines. [57]

The Byzantine victory over the Persian emperor, Khosrow II, was complete when Jerusalem was returned and the Church of the Holy Sepulchre once again came under Christian control. [58]

Thus, the victory of the Byzantines that Allah had revealed and the Prophet ﷺ had proclaimed occurred miraculously, as the verse says, within three to nine years.

---

55 "Heraclius;" http://en.wikipedia.org/wiki/Heraclius
56 "Heraclius 610-641;" http://fstav.freeservers.com/emperors/heraclius.html
57 Warren T. Treadgold, *A History of the Byzantine State and Society*, Stanford, California, Stanford University Press, 1997, pp. 287-299
58 http://web.genie.it/utenti/i/inanna/livello2-i/mediterraneo-1-i.htm;
http://impearls.blogspot.com/2003_12_07_impearls_archive.html;
http://en.wikipedia.org/wiki/Heraclius

The Opening of Makkah to Islam

When the Muslims had emigrated from Makkah to Madinah, the unbelievers made it very difficult for them to return and prevented them from performing their Hajj or 'Umrah. Furthermore, the unbelievers of Makkah repeatedly tried to attack the Muslims in Madinah, but were not successful.

About six years after the Hijrah, the Prophet ☀ had a dream that that he and some of his Companions were performing *tawaf* around the Kab'ah in *ihram* in complete safety and without fear of attack. The Prophet ☀ immediately announced this good news to his companions. Al-Bukhari narrates this story from Abu Musa about the Opening of Makkah:

> *The Prophet ☀ said, 'I saw in a dream that I waved a sword and it broke in the middle, and behold, that symbolised the casualties the believers suffered on the Day (of the battle) of Uhud. Then I waved the sword again, and it became better than it had ever been before, and behold, that symbolised the Opening (of Makkah to Islam), which Allah brought about, and the gathering of the believers.' (Al-Bukhari)*

As a help and support to the Prophet ☀, Allah revealed the 27th verse of Surat al-Fath in which He said that the dream was true and that, if He willed, the Companions would enter Makkah.

Allah has confirmed His Messenger's vision with truth: 'You will enter the Masjid al-Haram in safety, Allah willing, shaving your heads and cutting your hair without any fear.' He knew what you did not know and ordained, in place of this, an imminent victory. (Surat al-Fath: 27)

In Dhu'l-Qadah of 6AH, the Prophet ☀, together with about 1500 people set out towards Makkah in order to perform 'Umrah. This angered the idolaters of Makkah, who marched out to stop them. The Prophet ☀ and the Muslims went to a plain called Hudaybiyah to the north of Makkah and encamped there. The idolaters and Muslims entered into negotiations and a peace treaty called the Treaty of Hudaybiyah was signed. This allowed the Muslims, among other things, to return the following year in order to perform their 'Umrah in safety, as previously predicted in ayat 27 of Surat al-Fath.

In the *Tafsir al-Jalalayn*, this ayat is explained as follows:

> *In the year of Hudaybiyah before setting out, the Messenger of Allah* ﷺ *saw in a dream that he was entering Makkah, he and his Companions, and that they were shaving their hair and shortening it, and so he told his Companions about that and they rejoiced. So when they went out with him and the unbelievers blocked them at Hudaybiyah and they returned, then that was hard for them, and some of the hypocrites fell into doubt, it was revealed. ...* **'[He knew what you did not know and ordained, in place of this,] an imminent victory'** *which was the opening of Khaybar to Islam. And the dream came true the very next year.* [59]

The Opening of Egypt to Islam

> *Abu Dharr reported Allah's Messenger* ﷺ *as saying: You will soon conquer Egypt and that is a land in which the qirat* [60] *is named. So when you conquer it, treat its inhabitants well.* (Muslim)

In this hadith the Prophet ﷺ announced the coming opening of Egypt to Islam. At the time of the announcement, the Romans governed Egypt and the Muslims were not capable of taking on the Roman army. Yet these words of the Prophet ﷺ proved to be true. Not long after his death, in 641 CE during the caliphate of Umar ﷺ, the Muslims under the command of 'Amr ibn al-'As opened Egypt to Islam. [61]

The Taking of the Lands of Rome and Persia

> *Khosrow will die and then there will be no Khosrow after him. Caesar*

---

59 *Tafsir al-Jalalayn*, Faith Enes Publishing, İstanbul, 1997, vol. III, p. 1843
60 The people of knowledge say that the qirat is a sub-division of a dinar or a dirham
61 "The Arab Conquest of Egypt;" http://www.nationmaster.com/encyclopedia/History-of-early-Arab-Egypt

will die and there will be no Caesar after him, but you will distribute their treasures in the way of Allah. (Muslim)

The word *Khosrow* was the name used for the ancient Persian kings. The word *Caesar* was the designation of the Roman Emperor and after the fall of the Western Roman Empire only kings of Byzantium used this title. The Prophet announced in the hadith that the treasuries of these two kings would be in Muslim hands.

At the time of this announcement, the Muslims did not have the military strength or the economic and political organisation to achieve such victories, as the Persian and Byzantine Empires were very powerful. Nevertheless, events unfolded as predicted. During the Caliphate of Umar, Persia was defeated, bringing an end to the rule of the *Khosrows*.

Before the death of Heraclius, the Caesar of the time, in 641 CE, the treasury began to pass into Muslim hands during the caliphate of Abu Bakr. Many centres under the rule of the emperor were conquered, including Jordan, Palestine, Damascus, Jerusalem, Syria and Egypt. Constantinople was finally taken in 1453 by the Ottoman sultan, Fatih [62] Sultan Mehmed (Mehmed the Conqueror), in fulfilment of a hadith of the Messenger of Allah recorded by Imam Ahmad. Following the fall of the Eastern Roman Empire the title Caesar (*Qaisar*) passed out of use.

Thus, these major victories that seemed impossible to achieve, from the political and economic points of view, during the time of the Prophet all came about as miracles that Allah gave to Muhammad and his successors.

The Prophet's Announcement of the Death of the Persian *Khosrow*

In the course of his life, the Prophet delivered his message to rulers

---

62 "Fatih" means literally "Opener", just as "fath" means "opening", i.e. the opening to Islam.

and administrators by means of messengers and letters, calling them to submit to Islam. Historical sources tell us that some of them immediately heeded the call, and that others persisted in their denial, allying themselves with idolaters, hypocrites and unbelievers. One of the rulers that the Prophet ﷺ invited to accept Islam was the Persian *Khosrow* of that time, Parviz ibn Hurmuz. Muhammad ﷺ sent Abdullah ibn Hudhafah to him as a messenger. But Ibn Hurmuz rejected the Prophet's ﷺ message, displaying hostility toward the Muslims. He sent two messengers to tell the Muslims to submit to him. First, the Prophet ﷺ invited these two messengers to accept Islam; then he left them saying that he would inform them of his decision the next day. [63] The next day, the Prophet ﷺ gave the messengers this message that he had received from Allah:

> *Allah will send many tribulations to Khosrow by means of his son Shireveyh, who will kill him in such-and-such a month, on such-and-such a night, at such-and-such an hour! (Tafsir of Imam at-Tabari)*

He ﷺ also personally told them to tell the Persian administrator of the Yemen, Badhan, who had forwarded on the message of *Khosrow*:

> *Tell him that my religion and my empire will reach far beyond the kingdom of Khosrow; and say to him from me: 'Enter Islam, and I will confirm you in what you have, and I will appoint you king over the people of Yemen.' (At-Tabari)*

The ambassadors then returned to Yemen and described what had gone on. Badhan said: *'We will see what happens next. If what he said is true, then he is the Prophet whom Allah has sent.'* (At-Tabari) He then turned to his men and asked what they thought of him. The ambassadors had been greatly impressed by the Prophet ﷺ, and said: *'We never saw a ruler more majestic, more fearless and less guarded than him. He walked humbly amongst the people.'*

---

63 "Chosroes II, Siroes, and Prophet Muhammad (628 CE);"
http://www.cyberistan.org/islamic/chosroes.html

Badhan waited for a while and then he wanted to see whether or not what the Prophet 🌮 had said about Khosrow had come true. When he found it to be so, he announced that he was certain that the Prophet 🌮 was the Messenger of Allah. According to the hadith and other historical documents, Badhan had received a letter written by Khosrow's son, Shireveyh: *'I killed the Khosrow. When this letter reaches you, take the oath of allegiance from the people in my name. Regarding what Khosrow wrote to you, wait and do nothing until there is a new command from me.'* (At-Tabari)

When Badhan and his men calculated, they realised that all this had happened just as the Prophet 🌮 had said it would. [64] Badhan came to believe after that miracle, and he accepted Islam followed by the Yemeni Abna. [65] Badhan became the first governor appointed by the Prophet 🌮, and the first Persian governor to be a Muslim. [66]

Signs of the Last Day

There are also a number of predictions about events in the distant future that we can see unfolding even today, 1400 years after the Prophet 🌮 mentioned them.

> *Anas ibn Malik said, 'I shall tell you a hadith which I heard from the Messenger of Allah 🌮, and which no-one will tell you after me. I heard him say, "Among the signs of the Hour will be the disappearance of knowledge and the appearance of ignorance. Adultery will be prevalent and the drinking of wine will be common. The number of men will decrease and the number of women will increase until there will be fifty women to be looked after by one man."' (Reported in the two Sahihs from the hadith of 'Abd Rabbihi)*

---

64 Salih Suruc, *Kainatin Efendisi Peygamberimizin Hayati* (The Life of the Prophet [saas]), Yeni Asya Publications, Istanbul, 1998, p. 225
65 "Chosroes II, Siroes, and Prophet Muhammad (628 CE);" http://www.cyberistan.org/islamic/chosroes.html
66 Salih Suruc, *Kainatin Efendisi Peygamberimizin Hayati* (The Life of the Prophet [saas]), Yeni Asya Publications, Istanbul, 1998, p. 225

'Abdullah said, 'The Prophet ﷺ *said, "Just before the Hour, there will be days in which knowledge will disappear and ignorance will appear, and there will be much killing."' (Ibn Majah; also narrated by al-Bukhari and Muslim, from the Hadith of al-A'mash.)*

'Abdullah ibn 'Umar said, 'The Messenger of Allah ﷺ *came to us and said:*

"Assembly of Muhajirun, there are five things which if you are tried with them [then various types of punishment are going to happen to you] – and I seek refuge with Allah that you should come upon them:

If indecency appears among a people so much so that they make it public, plague spreads among them and illnesses that had never occurred among their predecessors in the past.

If they give short measure and weight, they are seized by drought and severe distress and the tyranny of the ruler over them.

If they refuse the zakah on their property, they are refused rain from the sky, and if it were not for the animals they would not have been given rain.

If they break the covenant of Allah and the covenant of His Messenger, Allah gives an enemy from outside of them authority over them, who takes some of what they own.

And as long as their rulers do not rule by the Book of Allah and make their choices on the basis of that which Allah has revealed, then Allah puts their fighting between them."'(Ibn Majah)

10. Conclusion

A miracle is an extraordinary event that is beyond the scope of human beings to perform. It can only be a sign from Allah. A miracle does not have to be simply an extraordinary physical event such as the parting of the sea (as granted to Musa ﷺ) or the ability to heal the blind (as granted to 'Isa ﷺ). Allah's support for His prophets, His revelations and His aid at times of crisis, no matter how small they may seem, are also miracles.

The Prophet Muhammad ﷺ was granted a range of miracles and these touched every aspect of his life. He was given exceptional miracles such as the Night Journey to al-Quds and the Ascent through the heavens, which while not witnessed by others, were supported by evidence they had to believe. He was given physical miracles such as the flowing of water from his fingers, which were witnessed by those present at the time. In addition, he was also granted knowledge of the Unseen through Divine revelation and helped against his enemies in various ways. In fact, everything about the Prophet ﷺ was unique and blessed, in his words, his prayers and his character.

The reasons for the miracles were as varied as the miracles themselves. Some miracles were designed to strengthen the resolve of the Muslims and to give them encouragement and support, both spiritually and physically. An example of this is the assistance that Allah gave to the Muslims at Badr. Some miracles protected the Prophet ﷺ from his enemies. These range from Allah revealing the plots and plans of the unbelievers to the Prophet ﷺ to actual physical support such as placing the spider's web at the mouth of the cave in which the Prophet ﷺ was hiding with his Companion from the unbelievers. Other miracles were given to show the Prophet ﷺ as a truthful person and to lend support to his message, for example the tree that testified to the Oneness of Allah and the Messengership of the Prophet Muhammad ﷺ. Miracles were also granted in response to requests from people. The people of Makkah had asked the Prophet Muhammad ﷺ for a miracle and thus Allah showed them the splitting of the moon.

Miracles have caused some people to come to faith, while others remained hard-hearted, attributing the signs of Allah to witchcraft and magic. It is within the power of Allah to show miracles that would make everyone believe:

> **If We wished We could send down a Sign to them from heaven, before which their heads would be bowed low in subjection. (Surat ash-Shu'ara': 4)**

However, this is contrary to the free-will that Allah has given us, which enables us to decide between right and wrong. In fact, a miracle is often a way to differentiate between those who truly believe and those who do not. Allah has told us in the Qur'an of the response of those who believe:

> **'Glory be to You! We have no knowledge except what you have taught us. You are the All-Knowing, the All-Wise.' (Surat al-Baqarah: 32)**

… and those who deny:

> **When they see a sign they only laugh with scorn. They say, 'This is just downright magic.' (Surat as-Saffat: 14-15)**

While the miracles granted to all the prophets were important, the miracles granted to the Prophet Muhammad ﷺ were different in one major respect – that they were witnessed by many more people. The miracles granted to 'Isa ﷺ and Musa ﷺ, for example, were witnessed only by those people that were present there at that particular time. However, the miracles of the Prophet ﷺ were more widely witnessed. Certainly those miracles that occurred in his lifetime were witnessed by those who were present, but he ﷺ left us with miracles that were witnessed even after his death, such as the prediction of the martyrdom of some of his Companions and the conquest of certain lands. However, the most enduring miracle, which has been witnessed by billions of people through the ages and throughout the world, is the Qur'an itself.

It is miraculous in the way in which it has been composed, in the way in which it has been revealed, and in the way in which it has been preserved.

The Prophet ﷺ has left us with the miracle of the Qur'an, exactly as it was revealed to him. With the free will that Allah has given, one can either respond with intelligence to this miracle by reading it and adhering to its commands or one can deny this miracle by abandoning it.

Those to whom We have given the book, who recite it in the way it should be recited, such people have iman in it. As for those who reject it, they are the losers. (Surat al-Baqarah: 121)

They said, "Glory be to You!
We have no knowledge except
what You have taught us. You are
the All-Knowing, the All-Wise."
(Surat al-Baqarah: 32)

JANNAH
The Garden from
the Qur'an and Hadith

ADEM YAKUP

Allah has created every human being to take delight in beauty and perfection. From the first moment we start to understand life, we feel a constant desire to attain this perfection. But no matter how much we may desire these things and no matter how great our effort to attain them, we can never attain perfection in this life. This is because Allah has created human nature to be content only in Jannah and it is only there that the desires of the heart can be fulfilled.